THE REFLECTING TEAM
Dialogues and Dialogues about the Dialogues

THE REFLECTING TEAM
Dialogues and Dialogues about the Dialogues

Tom Andersen

with contributions by
Arlene M. Katz,
William D. Lax,
Judith Davidson and Dario J. Lussardi

Foreword by
Lynn Hoffman

W. W. NORTON & COMPANY · NEW YORK · LONDON

Library of Congress Cataloging-in-Publication Data

Andersen, Tom.
   The reflecting team: dialogues and dialogues about dialogues /
Tom Andersen, with contributions by Arlene M. Katz . . . [et al.] ;
foreword by Lynn Hoffman.
     p.   cm.
   Includes bibliographical references and indexes.
   ISBN 0-393-70120-4
   1. Family psychotherapy.   2. Mental health care teams.
3. Communication in psychology.   I. Katz, Arlene Michele, 1946–
II. Title.
   [DNLM: 1. Communication.   2. Family Therapy – methods.
3. Professional-Family Relations.   WM 430.5.F2 A544r]
RC488.5.A473   1991   616.89′156 – dc20   91-27233

W. W. Norton & Company, Inc., 500 Fifth Avenue, New York, N.Y. 10110

W. W. Norton & Company, Ltd., 10 Coptic Street, London WC1A 1PU

1 2 3 4 5 6 7 8 9 0

dedicated
to
the shivering mountains,
the mystique of the light,
the touches of the winds
and
the joy of the water as it falls.

CONTENTS

Part III   Further Reflections

FOREWORD

One could call this a book but one could also call it the description of a new flying machine. When I first heard from the book's primary author, Tom Andersen, about the Tromsø team's idea of the reflecting team I was enchanted by its simplicity and stunned by its radical implications. I was once the interviewer in a family where a very angry and drunken father threatened to come back with a pocket full of stones to throw through the one-way screen. It never occurred to me to ask him and his family to change places with the team. But that is exactly what a reflecting team allows people to do.

In this sense, the invitation to change places is a statement that dramatically alters a family's position in relation to the professionals they have come to see. I sometimes talk about ways to "put the client on the Board of Directors." One family outreach worker I know invited representatives from a mothers group, whose families had all been troubled by problems of alcoholism or violence, to attend the annual banquet of the Board of Directors of her agency. They were asked to critique the services that they had received by recommendation of the court. They did so with great dignity, despite severe stage fright beforehand. These mothers, many of whom had been sexually abused, and some of whose children had been abused, have now been given a small grant by the agency to put together a handbook of child sexual abuse for other families like theirs.

The reflecting team is a similar concept. Families not only

experience it as empowering but also seem fascinated by the process of eavesdropping on conversations among professionals about themselves. Of course there are rules among the professionals about using positive descriptions and avoiding competitive or criticizing terms. Their comments generally offer new options and descriptions rather than ideas about what is wrong. It is paramount that people do not feel singled out for criticism or blame.

Those of us who began to experiment with this idea found more and more uses for it. I have begun to use a reflecting conversation in my teaching classes, asking small groups of five to discuss some topic or some case, in fishbowl fashion, with the rest of the group listening in. Then the larger group comments back about what they heard. The smaller group is asked to comment on the reflections in turn, or else we can turn back to what I call now a "free-for-all."

Some of my students became upset. They said, "This seems too artificial. What about open and honest communication?" I explained that if you don't set up rules against rivalry and negative connotation, people tend to compete against one another. The talkers in the group, whom I call the "Lions," begin to take all the space, and the "Lambs" get more and more silent. In fact, without interference, most classrooms will become divided into two species, which will soon begin to experience themselves as "smart" versus "dumb."

I further explained that the idea of "open and honest communication" is also an artificial structure, born of humanist psychology in recent decades. In many countries of the world — Korea, Vietnam, Puerto Rico — this type of communication is considered extremely disrespectful, especially in hierarchical relationships.

A similar factor that I stumbled on by accident was the shyness or feeling of being pressured that can be produced by direct gaze. I had asked a young woman therapist to present a case in front of a workshop group and I divided the participants into reflecting teams. I had asked them to talk to each other and not to direct observations to me or the therapist on the platform. Some forgot and began talking to us directly. Then I too forgot. At the end, unable to resist a "final comment," I turned to the therapist and made what I thought was a profound and interesting summary of her predicament. Then I sat back and waited for her to reflect back on what she had heard.

To my surprise, she looked very distressed and confused. She put her hands to her head and said, without looking at me, "I couldn't hear you, I couldn't hear you. When people talked to each other, I could hear, but not when they looked directly at me." She seemed very upset by her reaction, and needless to say, I was also upset. But that was a moment I never forgot. I began to see that the protected communication offered by the use of a reflecting team was extremely useful in giving people the freedom to accept or reject a thought or an idea, or even the freedom to hear it.

Let me offer one more illustration of the versatility of this concept. In a family outreach team I now consult with (People's Bridge Action, in Athol, Massachusetts), we have adapted a reflecting conversation to create what we call a "narrative model" for supervision. Instead of the usual problem-solving method in which everybody fires off suggestions to the person presenting a case, people go round the room in turn, offering associations from plays, movies, stories, their own lives or other cases. During this improvisatory process, each person has his or her own space bubble and may take as much time as he or she wants. Interruptions and cross talk are not allowed, and the original presenter speaks last as well as first. Then, if we want, we can go into the old style free-for-all. But often, the group wants to have another round of reflections, which then build upon each other in an unfolding and layering way, as whipped egg whites are folded into cake batter (apologies to those readers who have never made a cake from scratch). A capacity for metaphor, poetry and wit emerges, and the group is often surprised by the range of its own imagination. And a useful new idea for working with the case often emerges, although it is never clear how this comes about.

Perhaps the equalization between consultant and client is what most appeals to me about the reflecting team format. Even if people are asked to comment on the reflections but don't or simply make a few polite statements, an implicit respect for their expertise has been shown. In addition, the professionals expose themselves to the family in quite a new way. I'll never forget a time when I interviewed a therapist about a family in front of the extremely forward-thinking social work staff of a for-profit psychiatric hospital. The social workers were "allowed" to do family therapy but they had little say in the treatment plan for the patient. Here the psychiatrist was King (or Queen, as the case might be) and made all the clinical decisions.

In the case that was presented to me, the therapist described a ten-year-old girl who had become upset during some incident at home and had run off down the street crying. Her mother, acting like a good mother, had become alarmed and had taken her to see a psychiatrist. This doctor, because she was about to go on pregnancy leave, wanted to play it safe and recommended hospitalization. Once the girl was in a hospital, another psychiatrist interviewed her and gave her a diagnosis that automatically mandated a course of inpatient treatment for at least a year. For the next ten weeks, as was the rule for hospitalized children, the girl was forbidden to see her parents.

Since I was using a reflecting team format, I had asked to interview the therapist in front of the parents (the daughter, still hospitalized, was not present). I explained that the parents would act as my reflecting team. Although the therapist gave the family high marks for their cooperation, and mentioned how hard they had worked on their intensifying marital difficulties, the parents said they felt less optimistic. They blamed themselves for their daughter's condition. The mother, who had learned from the hospital reports that she was considered a "symbiotic mother," was feeling especially guilty. The father, after some initial reluctance, told of their intense despair. He said that they were given no information about their daughter's "illness" or about her recovery. They had no idea when she would be allowed to come home or in what way they could help her if she did come home.

I felt unable to comment and instead told about a time when I thought I would lose one of my own daughters. I said that the idea that one might have harmed one's own child was the worst fear that any parent could have. I also said that, just as in sudden crib death, these fears and the feelings of guilt and blame that go with them could severely stress the parents' relationship. The therapist also commented sympathetically, saying that he had no control over the hospital policy. When the couple left, I joined them in the hall and impulsively clasped the mother in my arms. I was unable to stop my tears, so I ducked quickly into the bathroom to repair my face. Afterwards, I met with the social worker, who shared his frustration at having so little influence over this particular case and privately criticized the way it had been handled.

What I was struck by was the way the use of the reflecting team allowed the parents to comment on, or at least raise some serious questions about, the handling of their own case. As these questions related to differences in the field regarding the diagnosis of mental illness and the treatment plans attached to those diagnoses, it was hard to answer them directly, especially in a private hospital setting. But I thought that, if I had gone in and interviewed the family as the outside "expert," as I used to do, I would never have elicited this feedback. The therapist and the social work staff, who were listening in, would not have heard it. And I would not have given the same message to the parents, which was: Your voices count. The most interesting comment they made, in fact, was when the father said to the therapist: You have often asked questions, but we have never heard questions being asked of you.

Another feature of the reflecting team is the rapidity with which people snap it up and use it. It seems to touch some nerve. The need for guidelines, such as this book delivers, is clear, given the popular appeal of the format and the likelihood that it may be used without sufficient training. Andersen's expansion of his group's initial insights about the "reflecting position," as they now term it, adds many important dimensions to the original idea. The chapter by Judy Davidson, William Lax, and Dario Lussard of the Brattleboro Family Institute is an eloquent and thoughtful description of how this format can be applied to a private practice group, not only in therapy but also in teaching and supervision. Finally, Arlene

Katz's "Afterwords" is a poetic statement that suggests how one might do a "follow-up" study using a reflecting position as inspiration.

A question people will ask, of course, is: Is this a new method? Is it a new school of family therapy? At this point, my answer would be "No." It enters the picture at a more general level of abstraction, at a level of therapeutic values and therapeutic stance. It offers a way of demedicalizing a profession that in its many manifestations – psychiatry, social work, psychology and all the branches of counseling – has been forced to deal more and more with objectively conceived assessments. These assessments have to do with degrees of individual pathology or type of family dysfunction. Labels based on these assessments (often dignified with the term "diagnosis") are often stigmatizing and usually pejorative.

Ben Furman, a psychiatrist in Helsinki, has written an as yet unpublished paper called "Glasnost in Psychiatry, Psychotherapy and Related Fields." He calls attention to the concealment of information from patients that routinely goes on, supposedly to "protect" the patient. In addition, clinicians often discuss cases among themselves in a manner which is prejudicial to the patient – but of course not within his or her hearing. Furman says that this practice, initially designed to protect the patient, often gives implicit license for what he calls "undisguised blaming." He feels that this is an oppression of the so-called mentally ill by the so-called mentally healthy.

The idea of the reflecting team comes at a time when many of us in family therapy, particularly those of us who have to deal with the new emphasis on criminality in families, are finding that we too are being co-opted as a vehicle for "undisguised blaming." The emergence of forms such as the reflecting team gives us hope that some correction to this situation may be at hand. For this reason, the publication of these papers is an important event, one that should be welcomed by every practitioner in the family therapy field.

Lynn Hoffman

INTRODUCTION

When Jürgen Hargens asked me to write this book, the cotter's spirit, which lives strongly in every Norwegian, instantly replied, "You are not able to do that!" And as always, the tendency was to agree with the spirit. When the cotter's spirit's reply had somewhat faded, a Norwegian fairytale came to my mind, a tale all Norwegians like. This story, like all Norwegian tales, changes with every teller.

It is about a king and his daughter, the princess, of whom he was very fond and proud because of her beauty and wisdom. What he liked the most was her laughter, impossible to define but full of pleasure. One day she could not laugh anymore. The king, desperate, declared that the man who was able to make her laugh again would be given a reward. The reward could be small or big, but so far it was not known. However, those who tried but did not succeed in making her laugh would have their backs sliced and salted.

Many young men came to the castle to try. Among them there were three brothers: Per, Pål and Espen Askeladd. The two first names are somewhat international, Per (Peter) and Pål (Paul) respectively, but Espen is purely Norwegian. The second name, Askeladd, translates into English as Ash-twaddler. Espen Ash-twaddler. He had his name because he liked to spend his days at the fireplace playing with the ashes, and thinking. His brothers, more efficient, mocked him constantly for that. When the two brothers, Per and Pål, took off for the castle they had trained themselves well: Per by reading a big book of laws, Pål by reading another big book that taught him all the Latin words.

They were stunned to see Espen following behind them. "Go home!" they screamed, "You will never make it!" Espen, ignoring his brothers' warnings, looked around curiously as he always did. As his eyes fell on a crow's wing, he cried out to his brothers, "I found, I found, I found a crow's wing."

"Throw it away," they said.

"No. One can never know for what it could be used!" he answered, and put it in his pocket.

Not long after he cried out again, "I found, I found an old shoe!"

"Throw it away; it is good for nothing," they said.

But Espen put it in his pocket, saying, "One can never know."

The third time he cried: "I found, I found a piece of red clay!"

"Ugh, throw it away," they replied again, but Espen put the clay in his pocket saying, "One can never know."

Per was the first one to enter the castle to meet the princess. He said, "It is hot in here." "It is hotter in the oven," she replied. Per, confused, couldn't speak and had his back inevitably sliced and salted. Pål said the same, he was similarly confused, and as he stumbled to find words, he was also taken away, sliced and salted.

When Espen entered and said the same, and the princess replied as before, Espen replied, "Good, then I can have my crow wing cooked." "What shall you use for cooking?" she asked. Pulling the piece of clay out of his pocket he said, "I will just wrap this around the wing!" "But the fat will leak out," she said. "No," Espen said, "I will collect the fat in this," and pointed to the old shoe.

The princess, dumbfounded, started laughing, as did the king and his servants. So, as promised, Espen Ash-twaddler had his reward.

Somewhere between definitely "No" and "One can never know," I said yes to Jürgen.

In the pages that follow, the reader will first be given a brief sketch of the context in which we work and live. This includes a brief overview of how the health services, particularly the mental health services, are organized.

Then you will be told about our way of thinking and working. This implies the constant interplay of what we learned by reading what others wrote, listening to and watching what others did and said when doing therapy, and how all of this changed us over time until we got where we are today.

This short history is followed by a summary of how we organize our work.

Finally, the reader will be given the opportunity to be acquainted with how our ideas have been applied to practical work, through clinical sketches and reports.

Chapter 4 presents a consultation with a system comprised of a couple and a general practitioner (GP). The GP and I made a team to reflect on the various definitions of the problems in the system.

Chapter 5 includes transcripts and summaries from a meeting, so that the reader may follow the conversation almost word for word, and see how the various conversations in the meeting reflect upon each other.

Arlene Katz, from Boston, interviewed four couples three months after these couples had been part of sessions (with American and Norwegian professionals participating) where the reflecting team was used. She encouraged the eight persons to recount their experiences and later personal reactions.

Members from the Brattleboro team in Vermont, who have applied these ideas in an American context, give an orientation about what they do in clinical work and in their training of family therapists.

In the final chapter, I discuss the changes that already have occurred since the start of writing this book. Additionally, there are some ideas about the possible evolution of the reflecting team.

ACKNOWLEDGMENTS

The reader will soon notice that ideas and practices sometimes are related to us (we) and sometimes to me (I). I use "we" to refer to my perception that the ideas and practices have emerged from the community of thinking and working that the Tromsø milieu represents.

Some people have been so important to the development of this project that I wish to mention their names. These people met every Thursday from 9 to 12 in the morning for work and discussion. Members of this group have been (listed in alphabetical order): John Rolf Ellila, Anna Margrete Flåm, Per Lofnes, Tivadar Scüzs, Finn Wangberg and Knut Waterloo. Another group has met Thursday afternoon between 1 and 4; the members were: Eivind Eckhoff, Anna Margrete Flåm, Magnus Hald, and Elsa Stiberg. I myself have been a member of both groups, which both started in January of 1984.

Sissel Falch Andersen's typing was an enormous help in making this book presentable. I thank her deeply for her work.

I am also very grateful to William Lax, who helped me correct the English text.

What I offer the reader are the pieces we collected on our walk – pieces that came out of the interplay of what we read, what we saw other clinicians do, and what emerged from our own intuitively created thinking and practice. Maybe the reader, walking with us while reading this book, will find something to be saved that later can be used differently from how we used it.

PREFACE

I have to thank Tom Andersen for his willingness to write down his story about the reflecting team – a therapeutic approach which has become well-known all around the world. Sometimes the idea of the reflecting team has been interpreted as a "method," but Tom Andersen makes it very clear that it is a way of thinking. (T)His way of thinking inevitably leads to this kind of practice, which is just one way of putting systemic ideas into action. Ideas change over time and they change with cultural differences. Tom is clear about this.

The context of Norway seems to be a major source for the development of the reflecting team. So, I am grateful that Tom writes about the context of his work – Norway and its political and mental health background. In doing so he brings forth the evolution of his thinking step by step.

Tom stresses that the ideas are not "his," but that they are part of the evolution of an ever changing group of people. And in just this way he unfolds the story – it is a narrative that depends heavily on its context. So, I like the way Tom tells the story and I have not tried to change his "Norwegian English" into some other kind of "English"; in this way some of the special flavor of the Tromsø team and their way of working has been preserved.

In traveling around, Tom has been part of the evolution of the reflecting team in other countries, especially in the USA. The Brattleboro team (Judith Davidson, William D. Lax, Dario

J. Lussardi) and Arlene Katz share some ideas about how the reflecting team "works" in quite a different context, pointing to various ways to put these ideas into action. There is *neither* the right *nor* the correct way in working; there is *both* one way *and* other ones. Tom reflects on our language – from "either-or" to "both-and," giving back to the customers their competence and their knowledge. For me this way of thinking-working entails some kind of deep respect for people based on some kind of ethics – an often neglected or overlooked issue when working "this way."

Jürgen Hargens

THE REFLECTING TEAM
Dialogues and Dialogues about the Dialogues

PART I

The Reflecting Team

1

THE CONTEXT AND HISTORY OF THE REFLECTING TEAM

Tom Andersen

NORWAY AND NORTH-NORWAY

Our country is long and thin like the branch of a tree. It curves slightly towards the east and is located between 58 and 71 degrees north latitude.

It is actually as long as the distance from the Canadian to the Mexican border, or almost as long as Japan. If the top of the country were rotated around its southernmost point, the country would reach as far south as Rome.

The land is divided by the Arctic Circle at 66⅔ degrees north. The part to the north is North-Norway.

Norway has four million inhabitants; three and a half million of them live south of the Arctic Circle, while half a million live in the northern arctic part. The country is divided into twenty counties; three of these are in the north: Finnmark, Troms, and Nordland. Each county is divided into communes. Norway has 454 communes with 99 in its northern part.

Norway's primary border is with Sweden. It borders on Finland in the north and also shares a part of its border with Russia. The front side is open to the sea, the North Sea in the south and the Arctic Sea in the north. The coast is torn by deep fjords. The land in the south has, behind the coastline, big and open valleys, where most of our common vegetation grows. In the north the land is mountainous, and in many places the sea meets the mountains with no land in between. The possibilities for plants to grow are limited.

The Gulf Stream, starting in the Gulf of Mexico, crosses the Atlantic and sweeps up the Norwegian coast, warming all of Norway. Our summers can be sweet and sunny, and our winters are not as harsh as those in Canada and Alaska, even though Norway lies as far north as those areas.

One big difference between the south and north in Norway is the shift of light from summer to winter. The south is more or less European, with days of normal length. However, in the north there are two months each of lightness and darkness. As the seasons shift, the light changes from the warm gold of summer to the deep, intense blue-gray of darker times. The south is calm and more or less predictable, but the north is very shifting and unpredictable. One never knows in the morning what the evening will bring.

The darkness and snowstorms in the winter give one much time for thinking followed by rethinking. Tours to the mountains in the middle of the still nights in light June encourage the expansion of ideas.

The population in the north stems from three groups of people: the Lap, reindeer nomads who were there first; "Norwegians" moving in from the south; and Finns coming in from Finland. Laps and Finns settle most often in Finnmark county.

In the past, going from southern to northern Norway was a major move. One could compare it to the westward journey of the early American settlers. People migrated north because of the rich fisheries.

During the last thirty to forty years, big changes have occurred. In the past, transportation was mostly by water, but today people travel more often on land or by air. As a result, people have moved from the coastal areas inland. Another reason for people's moves from the coast was the declining number of fish in the fisheries.

In the north people live in small places scattered over a wide area. The cities are small, with Tromsø, a center for trade, communications, and education, the largest one, with 50,000 citizens. This is where we work.

THE HELPING SYSTEM AND ITS PROVIDERS

The health and social services are organized according to the structure of Norwegian society: communes, counties, and the state.

On the commune level the so-called primary care is given. It includes care given by general practitioners, social workers, and public health nurses. People who ask for professional help are supposed to approach this "first line" of care initially. The communes are responsible for setting up such services and financing them. Considerable economic support is given from the state.

If the "first line" of care considers its competence to be insufficient, the "second line" is supposed to take over. This "second line" includes specialist services, either at out-patient clinics or in hospitals. These services are provided by the counties, which, like the communes, are economically supported by the state.

The state, besides being a money supplier, also has the responsibility of approving commune and county health-service plans. This assures that the services are as similar as possible all over the country. One-third of the Norwegian national budget goes to health and social services. This is one reason why taxes are so high in Norway. This, however, gives everybody guaranteed free services in hospitals.

Out-patient services, within either the first or second line, are to a great extent paid by a state insurance company. Every Norwegian has a pension at the age of 67 or a disability pension if disability occurs before the age of 67.

The psychiatric services, belonging to the second line of care, are mostly located in hospitals. There are two hospitals in North-Norway, one in Tromsø and one in Bodø. The Tromsø hospital serves Finnmark and Troms counties, and the one in Bodø serves Nordland county. There are newly established out-patient clinics in the local communities: three in Finnmark, four in Troms, and seven in Nordland. They are all recently founded and vulnerable because of staffing difficulties.

The staff at the various psychiatric services include: psychiatrists, psychologists, social workers, psychiatric nurses and regular nurses, mental health aides, occupational therapists, and physiotherapists. Most of the professional staff within the field of psychiatry are employed at institutions. Their salaries are fixed, and do not depend on how much they work. This is experienced as a great freedom, enabling professionals to devote as much time as necessary to a particular task.

The various health professions involved all have their own postgraduate educational programs. These various programs are defined by the corresponding unions, and the unions also give credentials when the formal requirements are achieved.

As you can see, most of the psychiatric care in Norway is performed in institutions, mainly in psychiatric hospitals. The various institutions (both in- and out-patient) are led by psychiatrists and rarely by psychologists. The content, defined by the Norwegian psychiatric association for their members, significantly influences all the other professionals' training and development.

According to Norwegian law, psychiatrists play a strong role in regulating the society's use of retention towards persons with deviant behavior. Both psychiatrists and psychologists who have passed the formal requirements may practice clinical work privately and are paid by the national insurance company. None of the other professions in the field of psychiatry can do so. Social workers, psychiatric nurses, mental health aides, occupational therapists, and physiotherapists can work only as employees paid by institutions led by psychiatrists or, in some few instances, by psychologists.

If one wishes to extend more services to meet people where they live, one must take the first line more seriously. In doing so, it seems best to invite more of them to cooperate with "the specialists" and to emphasize the development of techniques that are both simple enough to be grasped by those who do not work with psychiatric challenges every day and solid enough to provide help for those who ask for it.

OUR HISTORY

Even as we set 1974 as a starting point, we recognize that many ideas and experiences had been cumulating before that time. Most of us could not give up the premise that people up north, either healthy or sick, are strongly tied to the places they come from. We thought that the services should be located as much as possible within the local communities and should be congruent with the clinical challenges.

Some of us started to visit local communities and their professional staff members. Quite soon we understood that the way of working had to take new routes compared to what we were used to in the hospitals. We clearly saw that problems easily involved many people, both relatives and professionals. Therefore, we had to take both parts into consideration in the upcoming work.

1974-78

We were, therefore, well aware of the ideas of wholeness and relationship when in 1974 we started to meet informally, searching for new models of thinking and working. We greedily read Jay Haley's books, Salvador Minuchin's books and Paul Watzlawick et al.'s books, and stumbled forward with their ideas in our practical attempts. Our therapeutic successes were certainly few and small when they occurred. But our interests were ignited.

1978-84

I was offered the position of a professor in social psychiatry at the University of Tromsø. That became an important event, opening the way for two others: One was the organizing of a formal group of seven professionals* who aimed to work in close cooperation with the "first line" of care in Tromsø to prevent hospitalization of psychiatric patients. The other was the

---

*These were: Siri Blesvik, MHN, Birgit Eliassen, MHN, Anne Hertzberg, Ph.D., Aina Skorpen, MHN, Vidje Hansen, M.D., Odd Nilssen, M.D., and Tom Andersen, M.D.

participation of the same group in a two-year educational program in "systems-oriented family therapy" under the direction of the Norwegian Psychiatric Association and led by Philippe Caillé and his colleagues Charlotte Bühl and Håkon Hårtveit. Both events turned out to be significant.

The project of organizing out-patient psychiatric services in close cooperation with the "first line" of care was an experiment. The seven of us who took part decided to not have any facilities for ourselves. When we met the patients, we had to go to the offices of the first line. Working there, we asked the first line professionals to determine which patients they preferred us to see. We also said that they were welcome to "take the patient back," if they did not like our work. The professionals were invited to join the work as team members, if they wanted, but that was not a requirement.

If hospitalization was a natural outcome of the work, the "first line" people had to take the necessary steps; if medication was asked for, they made the prescriptions.

The hospitalization rate declined 40 % compared with a corresponding period before the project, and this decline was strongly related to the group's work (Hansen, 1987).

The "first line" of care liked this way of organizing the relationship between them and us, the "specialists," very much. They learned more about what specialists can do and what they cannot do. And they learned more about practicing psychiatry themselves. The established psychiatrists were much more reserved. When the group applied for funding to continue this work, the authorities rejected the application after having consulted the hospital psychiatrists. Relatively soon, all services returned to the old "normal" relationships between generalists and specialists, which meant longer distance and less communication.

We learned a lot from this experiment. We learned that our "systemic" thinking must also include ourselves and the relationships to other professionals of which we became a part. New ideas will grow unwillingly, if they are imposed from outside a system. Those ideas grow best with which the system itself (in this case the established psychiatric services) has come up.

Our beforehand belief that a community-based psychiatry might be a good solution became a conviction when we had to terminate the project. So we decided to search for another route.

The already mentioned educational program in family therapy brought us into contact with some of the people who set the tone in the family therapy field at that time. We met Lynn Hoffman from Ackerman in New York, Luigi Boscolo and Gianfranco Cecchin from Milan, and Phillippa Seligman and Brian Cade from Cardiff, Wales. The new attachment to the Milan approach gave some kind of detachment from the more structural and strategic styles we had tried to apply. What we found most relieving with the Milan style was the strong attention given to the ongoing interviewing process and lesser attention given to the interventions.

As the group that had worked on the initial project slowly fell apart, each of us continued clinical work in new settings, which gave some of us new possibilities for doing systems work. In this rather disruptive period, some of the seven of us thought that "going out" might be a good idea. We, therefore, started to arrange seminars in June every year, and as meeting places we chose remote places out in the communities. Guest speakers came from New York, Milan, Canada, Belgium, Rome, Texas, and surprisingly many professionals from all over North-Norway came to attend. Obviously, many wanted to learn more about systemic thinking.

The combination of listening to the visiting presenters during the day and rethinking the presented ideas during the light nights, undisturbed by a noisy surrounding society, seemed to fit the attending Norwegians very well.

1984–87

Several persons from the mental hospital in Tromsø participated in the June seminars, and some of them wished to start teamwork. That happened in January 1984. One team was comprised of social workers, psychologists, and psychiatrists from the out-patient clinic. The other team was comprised of young medical doctors and a social worker plus a psychologist. We tried to work the "Milan way."

Most of us had met with Cecchin and Boscolo and seen them working. We were struck by their cautiousness, as they gently put their questions or gave interventions. We had exactly the same impressions when the Ackerman team visited us. We not only were impressed by the gentleness, but also became more aware of the importance of giving much attention to the questions being asked.

The Milan team itself has emphasized the significance of the questioning (Selvini Palazzoli, Boscolo, Cecchin, & Prata, 1980, p. 12):

> The present phase of our research has brought us to face a new problem. Can family therapy produce change solely through the negentropic effect of our present method of conducting the interview without the necessity of making a final intervention? We hope this question will be answered after a significant number of family therapies have been conducted applying the above described method of interviewing and omitting any final intervention.

This was an issue to which we also had devoted some thought. Some of our reasons for doing so were our own feelings of not succeeding very well with the traditional Milan approach. We noticed that the interviewer almost never conveyed the ideas from his/her consultation with the team, neither in questioning nor when giving interventions. And we found it very difficult for the team to agree on *one* intervention. There was always a tendency for each team member to fight for his/her own interventory suggestion.

We were not very good at finding a smooth way out of this.

SOMETHING HAPPENED

I had been struggling with some ideas for two or three years together with my co-therapist*, but a lack of courage prevented me from bringing the ideas to light.

*The co-therapist was Aina Skorpen, MHN.

The therapeutic session was, as we saw it, in itself a process. And this process was meant to get the stuck process going again. So we thought it might be a good idea to let the "stuck" system see more of the therapeutic process. The thought behind this was simple, as we said that the goal is important but not the most important—most important is the way to the goal. When someone gets stuck it is often because it is hard and/or troublesome to find a way to get what he desires. The "stuck" ones say, "We don't know what *to do*." Could it be helpful for those who consulted us to see the way we work when we try to find contributions to a new route or more new routes to the goal?

It took us three years before we dared to let them see us work. It was so easy to think that usually, when we talked with people, we were loaded with too many nasty thoughts about them, which might "shine through" if we eventually spoke about them with them listening to us.

So this idea had a long gestation period. One day, however, in March 1985, the idea pushed for a birth.

A young doctor talked with a family who had a long period of misery. So much misery for such a long time that they did not know anything else but misery. We called him to our room and suggested some optimistic questions. He went back and tried, but the family easily took him back and down to their misery. We provided the doctor twice more with new optimistic questions—in vain.

Then the idea pushed hard to come out. We had noticed that there was a microphone in our room that was connected to loudspeakers in the family-interview room. It took us less than a minute to decide to knock at the door to the interviewing room and to ask them whether they wanted to listen to us for a while. The one of us who spoke said that we had some ideas which might be helpful for their talk. "If you find that idea of interest," he said, "we suggest that you all, both the family and the doctor, remain in your seats in this room. Our equipment allows us to dim the light here in your room, and we will turn on the light in our room. So you can see us, and we cannot see you anymore. We can also switch the sound so that you will hear us, and we will not hear you."

Our last chance to get out of this was that they would not agree, but they did.

And they seemed astonishingly excited. There we sat, listening to the funny sound when the light in our room came on, and thereafter the long, long silence.

One of us broke it with a stumbling word – something about endurance and strength. Another one followed with new words about the same issue. Someone came up with the idea that maybe all the struggle with the unkind destiny took the family members away from using the many unused possibilities they obviously had. Slowly we proceeded to a discussion about what might happen if some of these possibilities would be used.

When we turned the light and sound back on, we were ready to see and hear anything – from angry people to boring people.

What we saw were four very silent and thoughtful persons, who after a short pause started to talk to each other with smiles and optimism.

It felt very different from the usual way of working. The relationship with the family became very different from our relationships with the families with whom we worked in the "normal" way.

We certainly experienced the significance of Bateson's famous sentence, "The difference that makes a difference." We started to question our basic concepts and what they would be from now on. And even more important, how did we turn these concepts into practice?

The reversal of light and sound gave a surprising freedom to the relationship between us and the family. We were not *the* (only) responsible part anymore. We were only one of two parts.

This new format became known as the reflecting team. We thought of the French meaning of the word, not of the English one, which in our understanding comes close to replication. The French *réflexion*, having the same meaning as the Norwegian "refleksjon," means: something heard is taken in and thought about before a response is given. The reversal of light and sound also gave more freedom for thinking, and we started to ask how the various concepts and rules we followed affected *us*.

One early discussion was about hypotheses, particularly the hypotheses we were accustomed to making before we met with people.

Our understanding of the beforehand-information about a system would inevitably be within our context. In other words, our own context was the background for the information. Therefore, the hypotheses were at least to some extent close to where we were. And we started to wonder how close we were to those with whom we met. Or might it be that our hypotheses took us away from where they were? We decided to use as a starting point what the system itself defined as most relevant. One way to achieve this was to avoid having any ideas beforehand. Hypotheses were omitted if possible. However, sometimes it is impossible not to know something beforehand, and sometimes people feel offended if we do not receive the information beforehand. In such instances we received it, but we tried as hard as possible not to let that information be too much a part of us.

If a frame is given, as for instance a given hypothesis, the work will easily be similar to making quantification. The "thing(s)" in the hypothesis is either found or not found.

Bateson worried about such procedure (1978, p. 42):

> The ordinary processes of scientific advance in a lineal world, a world of lineal thought, are, after all, experiment, quantification, and, if you are anywhere within the realm of medicine, you will be expected to take a "clinical posture." And I want to suggest to you that experiment is sometimes a method of torturing nature to give an answer in terms of *your* epistemology, not in terms of some epistemology already immanent in nature. Quantification will always be a device for avoiding the perception of pattern. And clinical posture will always be a means of avoiding the openness of mind or perception which would bring before you the totality of the circumstances surrounding that which you are interested in.

If we were able to "tune" in on the ongoing and troublesome process of the stuck system, the pattern of that process might emerge by itself. Dealing with the words above, one could think of not only one pattern but two; the one is part of the stuck system, and the other pattern evolves in the new system, the stuck system plus us.

Although we did not know it at that time, in the spring of 1985, the reversal of light and sound turned around much of our former practice, which in the next run changed our understanding of what we might best do in therapy.

2

BASIC CONCEPTS AND PRACTICAL CONSTRUCTIONS

Tom Andersen

Looking back, it seems hard to say exactly which came first: what we did or what we thought. It seems fair to say that it has been a constant interplay between the stimulation from others' writings and clinical work and our own thinking and practical attempts. Our thinking and practice seemed to be much influenced by intuition. For reasons not very clear, we allowed ourselves to construct new routes the way we intuitively felt, and not necessarily the way the clear thought pointed.

It is important to emphasize that the concepts and formulations we began to rethink were far from being new. They had all been introduced before; however, at this point we had an opportunity to re-discuss their content so that they might be more helpful for and in our work.

We also allowed ourselves to relate to what we read with some freedom. We did not have to read and understand everything an author wrote. Sometimes we took out the bits that inspired us the most, and we permitted ourselves to understand what we read the way we understood it. In a way, we were in the position of understanding the author's understanding. That means that our understanding might be something very different from the author's understanding. In this way, reading never became any burden or anything we *had* to pursue.

The various central themes or concepts developed gradually. It might have been interesting for us to describe the sequence of our discussions but that is hard to figure out in hindsight.

I will, therefore, list the most important themes/concepts, discussing them in relation to our understanding of various writers' perspectives.

BATESON AND DIFFERENCES, AND DIFFERENCES THAT MAKE DIFFERENCES

Bateson (1972, 1978, 1979) brought to our attention that we do not see things as something in themselves. We see a thing as something different from its background. We make a "picture" of a man as something distinct from his background. The picture contains both background and man. Man himself sees and describes his background in terms of the differences he sees. He will be acquainted with his background in terms of differences he can see and hear and smell and touch and taste.

There are immanent differences in the background available for the searching senses. To define something as different from the surrounding Bateson calls "the making of a distinction." There are many distinctions that can be made. Think of all the distinctions just one sense can make; then contemplate what five senses can do!

There are so many differences available that one cannot possibly give attention to all of them. This is certainly so when the background is constantly shifting, as happens in interchanges between two or more persons. Making a picture of a situation is to make certain kinds of distinctions. Since there are always more possibilities for making distinctions, the picture one holds is a result of the distinctions the describer makes.

In other words, there is always more to see than one sees.

Therefore, there are many un-made pictures (moving pictures) of various situations. And, maybe even more important, two persons will most probably make different distinctions of the same available situation or different "maps" of the same "territory," as Bateson said.

Many people have not grasped Bateson's idea. They believe that there is one correct history and one correct picture. If one thinks this way, one can easily become involved in heavy discussions or even fights about who remembers correctly or who sees correctly.

Those following Bateson's idea might be intrigued by what they heard that another person saw or heard or smelled or tasted or touched in the situation – things which s/he did not notice. These new aspects of the moving "picture" of the situation could stimulate differences in his/her own evolving "picture." And these differences contribute to the person's shading his/her moving picture.

In short, this leads to Bateson's famous sentence: "the elementary unit of information – is a difference that makes a difference" (1972, p. 453). The verb "to make" in the last sentence induces the idea that the difference that is made is made by a difference over time. Bateson says a difference over time is a change.

In short, there are two different meanings in Bateson's use of the word *difference*: First, something is distinct in its being different from its background, and second, a change is a difference *over time* brought about by a difference. These ideas have become an important basis for clinical work. The Milan associates' interview contains a lot of questions searching for differences when situations around a problem are described. The Milan group itself has described their questions (Selvini Palazzoli et al., 1980), and Peggy Penn (1982) has independently described their questioning. Questions that often clarify problematic situations are those that comprise comparisons and relationships. Questions that search for differences that make differences are those that focus on the changes, e.g., how can this be explained?

BÜLOW-HANSEN AND THREE VARIANTS OF DIFFERENCES

I had the privilege of following the work of two Norwegian physiotherapists, Aadel Bülow-Hansen and Gudrun Øvreberg, the former the teacher of the latter (Øvreberg & Andersen, 1986).

Over the last 40 years Bülow-Hansen has developed a physiotherapeutic method for persons who suffer from muscular tension, which often is part of a more comprehensive pattern of tension. Very early, she focused on breathing, and saw breathing and moving of the body as two inseparable aspects. The ongoing breathing cycle, from inhalation to exhalation to inhalation and so on, is coherent with corresponding movements of all muscles throughout the body, even if the eye does not notice it.

In other words, the inhaled air "goes" to the outmost fingertip and toe. For various reasons muscles become tense, which prevents the air from moving through that part of the body. In other instances, the whole chest becomes tense, thus preventing the flow of air. That happens when, for various reasons, a person tends to limit his/her expressions. Emotions and words following the exhaling air.

Sometimes a person experiences that the circumstances do not welcome all kinds of utterings from him/her. One way to prevent such expressions is to limit the breathing excursions. And one way of restraining the exhalation is to limit the act of inhalation. A Norwegian word for inhalation is inspiration. One could literally say that the rather tense circumstances make the person reduce his/her inspiration from the surroundings.

One way of limiting the inhaling movements is to use those muscles of the body that have a flexing function. These are the muscles that bend: neck, elbow, shoulder, hip, front side of the torso, knee, etc. Increased activity of these bending muscles will simultaneously act on the chest so that its movements become limited. In addition to these bending muscles one should not forget all the small mimic muscles all over the face and the muscles all around jaw, tongue, and front neck. Those of these muscles which are also bending ones have a tremendous limiting effect on the chest's movements when they are activated.

Bülow-Hansen's hands negotiate with the bending muscles, e.g., those in the calf. In doing so the working hand induces pain. The pain stimulates an extension of that part of the body, which in turn stimulates inhalation. And if the body is ready for it, the exhaling phase will be followed by reduced tension in the calf muscle. This opens up possibilities for the stretching muscles (the extensors on the front side of the leg) to extend the knee. As this extension is held for a while, deeper inhalation occurs. And actually a vicious cycle takes place. The stretching stimulates inhalation, the inhalation in turn tends to stimulate more stretching, which in turn stimulates inhalation. These mutual activities continue until the chest is filled according to what its flexibility accepts.

When the exhalation lets the air go, this tends to decrease the tension all over the body. As her hands work, Bülow-Hansen's eyes follow the breathing response all the time. If her hands induce too much pain or her stretching of the various parts of the body becomes too energetic, the body responds with a tendency to stop the breathing movements.

All the time her eyes tell her how strong the stimulations of her hands can be and how long she can stimulate. At the slightest sign of restraining chest movements, she lets her hands go. Thus she works from the legs to the abdomen to the shoulders, then to the neck, jaw and face, particularly including the areas around the eyes. The lesson this method taught me was that the hands' stimulations had to be strong enough to make a breathing response. If they were too small, nothing would happen. However, if the hands were too strong or held too long, the breathing tended to stop by the chest tightening up.

One variation of Bateson's "difference that makes a difference" came out of this: there are three types of differences but only one of them makes a difference, namely the appropriate different one. When we applied this to the conversations we took part in as therapists, some main guidelines emerged. Shifting the word difference to daily language, I chose the term "unusual." If people are exposed to the usual they tend to stay the same. If they meet something un-usual, this un-usual might induce a change. If the new they meet is very (too) un-usual, they close up in order not to be inspired. Therefore, what

we, their supposed helpers, should strive for is to provide something unusual but not too un-usual in the conversations that
we take part in with these people. This is a rule that comprises
the setting in which we meet, the themes or issues the conversation covers, and the way or the form the conversation takes.

BEING ONESELF

For a long time we viewed a person as part of one or more
relationships. We still do, but our perceptions have somewhat
changed. Earlier we saw him/her as being influenced and
changed according to the dynamics of the relationships. In
other words, the relationships were "in charge" of the person.

Maturana's (1978) and Varela's (Maturana & Varela, 1987)
writings have been most helpful for us in coming up with our
recent thoughts on this topic. Bülow-Hansen's work has been
helpful too.

Maturana and Varela speak on the basis of a biological understanding that a person is strongly structurally determined.
These biological structures are, however, continually changing.
Every cell of the body rebuilds itself all the time. In this process it conserves the basic functions that enable it to adapt to
its immediate surrounding – to other cells and to the fluid that
circumscribes the cell. This environment tends to shift over
time, but the cell holds a variety of functionings in order to
adapt to these changes. Additionally, by rebuilding itself the
cell might also expand its mode of functioning as a response to
changes in the surroundings.

Maturana and Varela use this principle also in considering
the whole person. Our understanding of this is that at a certain
point in time a person can only be just this person s/he is. This
means that s/he can only react to a certain situation in one of
the ways s/he has in his/her repertoire. This repertoire, however,
may be changed over time by some old ways fading out and
some new ones emerging.

If a situation brings a perturbation (one might say a disturbance) to which the person cannot react because of a lack in his/
her repertoire, s/he can only react in one of two ways. S/he can

close up from the disturbance, thereby protecting himself or herself, or using Varela's and Maturana's words, conserving the organization s/he represents. In clinical terms that would be to conserve his/her integrity. Or, if s/he allows such alien perturbation to enter the organization s/he represents, s/he disintegrates. One might say that the disintegrating disturbance has been too different with respect to the repertoire of the person.

When a person closes up in response to a disturbance, this could also be seen as a response to something that is experienced as being too unusual. The signs Bülow-Hansen looks for in order to know whether her hands disturb appropriately unusual are the breathing movements of the chest. She can also watch for an indication in the bending muscles, which may increase their activity. If the hands tend to bypass the limits of the appropriate usual to the too unusual, the breathing becomes restrained and the bendings of the muscles can be seen — the hands close, the arms may cross, the face wrinkles, etc.

All these signs can actually be noticed if a conversation contains something too unusual. In addition, one might notice that the person becomes less attentive and thoughtful and the responses become more reserved. In order to stay in a conversation with a person, one must respect the person's basic need to conserve his integrity. In order to be able to do that, one has to learn to be sensitive to his signs, which often are very subtle indications that our contributions to the conversation have been too unusual. One thing that helps to see these signs is going slow when talking with people, i.e., going so slow that they have time to let us know their responses, and we have time to notice them.

RELATING TO OTHER(S)

Every person I meet has a major interest in conserving his integrity throughout the meeting. What I say and what I do determine his being open for a conversation or his closing up. When I am observing him, he actually observes my observing. We are both in an observing position. I observe whether there are signs which indicate that I have become too unusual. By observing his responses to my observing I can indirectly become an observer of my own observing. He observes in order to define who I am, in order for him to know how much he dares to engage in the conversation while conserving his integrity. He is making a picture of me, a moving picture, and he gives that picture an explanation that tells him what he might expect from me. That explanation will guide his sayings and doings towards me in his relation to me.

One important consequence of this perspective is that it makes clear that one person actually is many persons. S/he becomes one person in one circumstance, another person in another circumstance. However, all these different persons come out of the same person who has some basic characteristics that make him *that* person. So it is equally right and wrong to say that one person is many persons or to say that all these different persons are the same person.

A simple drawing of this process of mutual signs of observing may serve to clarify these ideas:

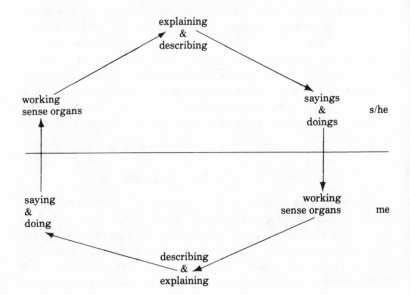

The process presented in this drawing is exactly what we have understood as "an observing system," which Heinz von Foerster has written about (1979).

Some Language Difficulties

When a word is said it is passed from a speaker to a receiving listener. The word has a meaning for both of them, but does it have the same meaning for both of them? We have to consider the possibility that meanings differ.

Actually there is a difficulty on this very particular point, because as a writer I have to ask whether I have the same meaning of the word "meaning" (as it is written just here) as you, the reader of this written word. If I try to clarify my meaning by using other words, the problem still exists in the sense that the new words may hold different meanings for me and the reader.

Basic words in this book are *idea, description, explanation, meaning,* and *understanding.* Let us look at my understandings of these words.

I see an *idea* as a glimpse of something; it could be a glimpse of a description or a glimpse of an explanation or a glimpse of a meaning, or a glimpse of something else. A *description* can be understood as a more firm "picture." This "picture" should be regarded as a moving picture. It contains all the qualities that correspond to the senses of seeing, hearing, smelling, tasting, touching and also sensations from the "inside" of the body (the so-called proprioceptive stimuli).

Explanation is regarded as how the "picture" can be understood. A *meaning* comprises description and explanation but it is something more. It carries with it that the description and explanation have a certain meaning for the person. This meaning becomes the basis for how the person relates to the "thing" that is described and explained in terms of some kind of acting. The content of the word understanding comes close to meaning. In this book *definition* is regarded as description plus the explanation. So meaning is something more than definition—it is the definition plus a personal component of the definer.

Responsibility

The reader will now be taken on a short side-track to deal with the phenomenon of responsibility.

To what extent am I responsible for my opening up my sense organs and thereby being perturbed by that which "touches" me? Most likely, I am responsible for my descriptions and the meanings I give to my descriptions. I am also responsible for all my doings and sayings. To what extent can I be responsible for the other person's opening up for my disturbing her or him? Most likely, I cannot be responsible for the description and the corresponding meaning s/he makes, and I cannot be responsible for the sayings and doings s/he presents to my sense organs. These questions and ideas deserve to be pursued.

THE ACT OF DESCRIBING AND EXPLAINING HUMAN ACTIONS AND HUMAN INTERACTIONS

Whenever a person describes another person, s/he is part of an observing system. In other words, what can be described and what is available for observation and description from moment to moment are determined by the observing system. The observer or the person being described limits his/her sayings and doings according to his or her understanding of the relationship with the describer. However, what becomes available is so rich in details that one person cannot give attention to all of it. One has to select something for one's attention. Thereby, something will be focused on, and something will be left out. In Bateson's and in Maturana's terms this focusing of attention is called "making a distinction."

This making of distinctions is an act of the describer. And this act certainly has to do with the describer's interests, knowledge, history, etc. The main point here is that two different describers in the same situation will probably make different distinctions, and therefore will come up with different descriptions, inevitably leading to different explanations of the described.

One important point to remember is that in every act of

description many other possible descriptions are left out, since many possible distinctions have not been made. One should also remember that the main way of drawing distinctions during a dialogue is to ask questions, which leads to just this question: "What would my descriptions be if I asked all the questions I did not ask?"

As we understood them, Maturana and Varela (1987) called various phases of this process *names* (verbs), *knowing* (corresponding to describing and explaining), and *acting* (sayings and doings).

One part of the acting was the acting upon which surrounded the sense organs, e.g., the opening or closing of the eyes. For the purpose of this discussion I like to introduce the word *sensing*. This covers three steps: sensing, knowing, and acting. What fascinates me as I read Maturana and Varela is their making sensing-knowing-acting a coherent whole. This whole fulfills two requirements: (1) conservation of the organization and integrity of the person, and (2) participation in the interplay with the surroundings.

The sensory cells cannot not activate the brain cells which cannot not activate the muscles, and vice versa. It is a whole. However, the routes from the sensing "side" to the acting "side" may be many. There are various ways in a very rich repertoire of possibilities.

Every brain cell connects to many other cells, both receiving "influences" from many other cells and further influencing many other cells. The influencing might be either inhibiting or activating. One can never predict which route the process will take. Von Foerster says, according to my understanding, that, as the process proceeds towards the acting, it partly changes the processing medium itself, i.e., the brain, (Segal, 1986).

One important thing to think of is that the brain is constantly in action, so that influences from the sense organs modify an already ongoing process in the brain. It has been compared with a room crowded with talking people. If a person from outside opens the door and speaks, the speaking is analogous to the influence from the sense organs. The ongoing talking activity in the room is changed only to a small extent by the talking from the door. As this flow passes through the brain, one might consider the possibility that the knowing part processes a clear description and a corresponding clear explanation. But one might also expect the possibility of almost no or only vague descriptions, so that the person is not able to fully understand the surroundings and the disturbances it brings to the person.

One can also think that even if the meaning is unclear the acting goes on. The body works without the mind's noticing it. I am very often struck by how easily people with bodily complaints accept this saying: "Sometimes a person engages himself in a situation that at this point in time represents something that the person is not ready to take part in. The mind has not yet been able to understand what this might be. But the body has. The body gives its signs that there is something in the situation the person should be protected from at this point in time. The body has grasped the idea about this, which the mind has not yet."

MULTIVERSA RATHER THAN UNIVERSUM AND (OBJECTIVITY)

An important summary of what has been said so far is that the describer of another person is, by his/her participation in the observing system, influencing what can be observed and described. By making descriptions, the describer draws some particular distinctions, thereby leaving out all other possible distinctions. The descriptions and the corresponding explanations will therefore be closely connected to the describer's acts. And finally, the person's inner neurological make-up and its function will influence the act of describing and explaining.

This leads us to conclude that to a large extent any description or explanation is observer-dependent and each person describing the same situation will come up with one version each; when these versions are compared, they will be somewhat different. No description is better than the other ones; they are equally "valid." The consequence for clinical work is that we must search for and accept all existing descriptions and explanations of a situation and promote further searching for more explanations and more definitions not yet made.

Each person has a perception (we may call it a constructed perception) of the situation to which the person "belongs." This perception is that person's "reality." Another person in the same situation also has a perception of "reality," but that "reality" is that particular person's "reality." "Reality" exists only as a perceiver's "reality." The same "outside" situation may turn out to be(come) many "realities." No "reality" can be said to be better than the other ones. They are all equally "real."

The picture of "reality" fits in such a way that the person can survive in that "reality." Ernst von Glasersfeld expresses it this way (Segal, 1986, pp. 86–87):

> Radical constructivism is less imaginative and more pragmatic. It does not deny an ontological "reality"—it merely denies the human experiencer the possibility of acquiring a true representation of it. The human subject may meet that world only where a way of acting or a way of thinking fails to attain the desired goal—but in any such failure there is no way of deciding whether the lack of success is due to an insufficiency of the chosen approach or to an independent ontological obstacle. What we call "knowledge," then, is the map of paths of action and thought which, at that moment in the course of our experience, has turned out to be viable for us.

TWO INTERPLAYING DIALOGUING PROCESSES

From Circular to Elliptical Dialogues

Relating comprises sensing, knowing, and acting. A new drawing will hopefully serve the purpose of simplicity:

The drawing indicates an ongoing "inner" process which might be regarded as a circle. The "inner" process partly serves the conservation of the person's integrity but also serves as a basis for the expansion of the acts of sensing, knowing, and acting.

The condition necessary for this expansion is the connection of this "inner" process with an ongoing "outer" process of exchanges which occurs when one takes part in relationships with others, as indicated in the following drawing. According to this, one might say that two "inner" processes and one "outer" process are occurring in parallel when two persons encounter each other.

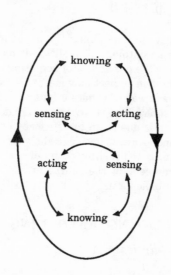

If this encounter is a dialogue, e.g., therapist and client engaging in conversations during "the talking cure," it might be of importance to think of three parallel conversations going on at the same time: two "inner" talks and one "outer." The "inner" talk seems to serve at least two aims: dealing with the exchanged ideas and dealing with the person's participation in the "outer" talk.

Part of the "inner" talk is about what the meaningful content of the "outer" talk is and also: *how* can this "outer" talk be best performed? It looks as if a person constantly talks to her/himself about how s/he can be connected through a conversation in order to achieve new and helpful perspectives (descriptions and explanations) without the person's integrity being offended.

When we take part in the "talking cure" we should probably ask ourselves all the time: is the talk I have with this person slow enough so that the other person and I have time enough for our "inner" talks?

If the reader goes back to the last figure with the words knowing, acting and sensing, s/he may notice that its shape is like an ellipse. An ellipse has two centers, one at each end, and it is in itself the mathematical expression for the line around the two centers. So I wondered whether we should challenge the notion of circularity by calling a conversation an elliptical exchange of ideas?*

For some time Stein Bråten, a Norwegian sociologist, has discussed the "inner talk." He sees a person as two parts; one is "I" and the other is the "virtual other." The two parts share different perspectives through their dialogues. Bråten came to this idea by a different route from the one we have taken. He refers to Gadamer, who cites Plato's notion of thought as the inner dialogue of the soul with itself, to Piaget, who calls this "egocentric speech," and to C.S. Peirce, who said that one reasons to persuade the critical self.

Change Can Be Limitation and Change Can Be Evolution

The first change relates to a person's acting (behavior) when this (change) is instructed or imposed from outside. The other change comes from inside where the acting's (the behavior's)

---

*These have been ideas my friend Ebbe Reichelt, a Norwegian theologian and teacher, and I played with in May '88. The ellipse is the area that is brought forth when a cone is truncated obliquely. Stars and suns and other celestial bodies move in elliptical orbits.

premises, namely the knowing and the sensing aspects, are widened.

The first way will easily be experienced by the one acted upon as a threat to his/her integrity. In order to defend one's integrity, the person closes off from this imposing or instructing act from outside. In this process of closing off, the person limits the use of her/his repertoire of acting (behaving). This limitation may satisfy the instructor if the limitation stops the behavior the instructor has defined as deviant or unwanted.

Here the important point to note is that instructions easily contribute to the limitation of the repertoire of acting and thereby the corresponding aspects of knowing and sensing. Such changes of restraint, which are more or less predictable, correspond to the idea that a person can be steered by another. Such instructions lead to intimidation, which is very different from intimacy.

The second kind of change occurs when there is freedom for exchanges of ideas between two or more persons, securing both or all persons' individual integrity. Under such circumstances new ideas of knowing or sensing or acting or new ideas for using the possibilities which one's repertoire already holds might emerge. Having the character of evolution, such changes cannot be predicted, neither with respect to what they will be nor when they will occur. These changes know their own route and own time. Briefly spoken, a change can be of two kinds: it can either limit or expand the ability to describe and explain and act.

An example may clarify this point. A little baby moves all of his/her body when s/he laughs. The laughing movement goes out in all the body, even the toes. The toes laugh. As the child grows and starts walking, the upright position limits the possibility for the toes to take part in the laughing movement. When the child grows even bigger, s/he is taught that certain ways of laughing are more appropriate than others. When s/he becomes an adolescent, s/he may start to learn that there are things one does not laugh at, and even smiling declines.

The point here is that we all, including the reader, still have the potential to let the laughing movement reach and also move the toes. The possibilities only tend to be limited over time, as habits, customs, etc., are introduced. We also have the potential for even greater restriction of the laughing movement. If an unpleasant person is around, it might happen that our smiles, which previously have reached the eyes, come to stop at the lips. The unused smiles and laughs lie there, sleeping, waiting for an outburst.

How can we create a coming-together that makes such outbursts possible? Not rarely, words and questions do become a circumstance for such. The good circumstances may loosen up all the available laughings, even those of the toes. And exchanges of ideas with others may create other and new forms of laughing, e.g., through writing or painting or singing.

Saying "No" Is Fundamental

Since the too unusual might threaten a person's integrity, we find it of utmost importance to organize our work in such a way that those who come to talk with us have an ongoing opportunity to say no to a conversation's form, its content, its context, or to all of this. The best way to be sure that there is no unspoken "no" is to let the discussion about the ongoing conversation be a part of the dialogue. Using words such as "like" and "comfortable" in our questions might help the process, e.g., "How would you like to use this session?" and "What would you feel most comfortable with?"

Every conversation challenges our sensitivity to pick up all the small cues in the words or all the small bodily utterings which are signs of something in the conversation the person does not like or does not feel comfortable with.

CONVERSATIONAL EXCHANGES

We see conversations as the important source for the exchange of appropriate different descriptions and explanations, definitions and meanings. Such exchanges might color old descriptions and explanations, and even lead to the emergence of new descriptions and explanations. Thus, this provides the broadest possible basis for what a person might choose in order to handle stuck situations differently or to respond to new events, be they foreseen or unforeseen.

There are so many similarities between the exchanges of conversation of a fellowship and the exchanges of breathing of an individual that I let the understanding of the one kind of exchanges inspire the understanding of the other. In other words one serves as a metaphor for the other. One thing I like to say is that a fellowship depends on conversation in order to survive, just as the individual depends on breathing to survive.

Looking at the curve of the respiratory cycle as it is transformed to paper, one sees the rising part indicating inhalation and the falling part indicating exhalation. Between these two parts there are some small pauses, a small pause before inhaling starts and a small pause before exhaling starts.

During the cycle of conversation one also needs a small pause before talking (acting) and a small pause before listening (sensing). The pause before talking might be used to ask oneself, "What did he really say?"

Harold Goolishian from the Galveston Family Institute in Texas, whom we have been in touch with quite a lot, always says: "You should listen to what they really say, and not what they really mean."

The pause before talking could also be used to ask oneself: "What of that which I heard him saying intrigues me the most?"

The pause before listening could be used to ask oneself: "Has what I said been appropriately unusual or too unusual?"

Conversations need pauses, enough for the thinking about the process of the conversation to take place. And they should be slow enough to let the mind select those ideas it likes to be attached to, and to find the words that can express that attachment. A conversation should struggle to include the two or more participating persons' talking and thinking and listening in terms of speed and rhythm of these phases. When we talk with someone, we try to follow his/her rhythm without losing our own.

In this respect, two articles on the physiology of breathing offer very interesting ideas. Southerland, Wolf and Kennedy state (Christiansen, 1972, p. 26):

> It seems remarkable . . . that records [of the breathing cycles] taken three to twenty-eight days apart, can reproduce each other with such precision. Yet this is the fact in each case. If duplicate records, taken days apart in several hundred cases, are shuffled, they can be paired quite easily. Consequently we have come to call these spirometric pictures "fingerprints" records of our patients. These records could not be duplicated by any conscious process.

And Alexander and Saul state (Christiansen, 1972, p. 26):

> Comparing a series of curves of one individual with a series obtained from another individual, two facts are immediately apparent. The first is that the curve is rather typical of the individual, like his handwriting. In other words, there are characteristic differences between the respiratory patterns of different individuals, just as their handwritings are different. In our series, no two individuals have yielded identical respiratory patterns.
>
> The second fact is the constancy of any individual's respiratory tracing. In about three-quarters of the cases, despite variations in detail, the major features remained characteristic of the individual over long periods (at least three years). Those which showed considerable variability still retained recognizable individuality. Experiments showed imitation of another's spirogram to be extremely difficult.

From this I extracted that, even if there is great stability in the rhythm of breathing, over time there is a tendency toward change in this rhythm.

Maturana speaks of the tendency of various parts of the body to stay the same or shift over time. Some parts are very stable, e.g., the genes. Some are less stable. Maybe the breathing belongs to the more stable ones over time?

Using breathing as a metaphor, we become aware that we have to follow another person's speed and shifts through her/

his listening, thinking, and talking. If not, the conversation might suffocate.

WHICH OF OUR TALKING CONTRIBUTIONS ARE MOST HELPFUL?

What is most helpful for people who see themselves in a "stand-still" situation? We can give explanations and advice. We can even say that people ought to receive our interpretations and advice. We might even persuade or push or threaten people to receive them. This might be a dangerous route for the relationship of which the conversation is a part. As already mentioned, Maturana's (1978) concept of instructive interaction will most probably be of some help for us.

Advice and interpretations might easily become alien perturbations for the person. If s/he "takes in" something for which his/her repertoire has no response, disintegration might take place. One way to avoid such happening is to end the relationship. Much influenced by the Milan team's questions, Penn's writings about questions (1982, 1985), and all the discussions with Harold Goolishian and Harlene Anderson about questions, we find it safer to use questions only. There are certain exceptions to that rule, namely, when it would be too unusual for those we speak to if we did not give advice or did not make interpretations.

Appropriately unusual questions which raise the possibility of more than two answers ("yes" and "no") most often open up to more questions. We basically find our contributions to be questions, especially questions that those we speak with usually do not ask themselves, and which give possibilities for many answers, which in turn might create new questions.

WHICH OF OUR LISTENING AND THINKING CONTRIBUTIONS ARE MOST HELPFUL?

Again I prefer to quote Harold Goolishian, who has repeatedly said, "Listen to what they really say!" We can be sure that what they say includes invitations to what can be talked about.

We prefer to continue the talk about something that is strongly connected to what they just said – in other words, what they just invited us to talk more about.

When they talk I think about the words they use, as well as the tone and bodily movements that follow the words, and I ask myself which of all that I hear is the most important to talk about more. These most important parts we call "openings." I ask myself, "Which opening shall I relate my questions to? E.g., shall I ask for more clarification of the words, or shall I ask for the history or the circumstances that represent the context, or shall I ask what might happen if there were shifts in the ongoing actions in the situation?"

When I ask them questions I simultaneously ask myself the question: "Can I see any signs expressed by them which indicate that I am too little unusual, or are there any signs that I am appropriately unusual or are there signs that I am too unusual?" I also prefer to ask myself, "What about the speed for this conversation, and its rhythm?"

I also ask myself, "Does this conversation include any issues that I myself am not ready to talk about? Does the conversation take a form I am not ready for? Do I start to get hung up on my own meanings about how the situation should be described and explained? Do I even come up with meanings about how the situation should be solved?"

If I give a "yes" to any of these questions, I need a longer, undisturbed pause to think more about my own contributions to the conversation. For example, if I start to have meanings that guide my participation in the conversation, I need someone's help to ask questions about my meanings and my act of making meanings.

EXCHANGES

We think of the usefulness of seeing a conversation as a series of exchanges of ideas. Something said is listened to, thought over, and a question is created that hopefully creates new ideas about what has been said first. The stuck ones know exactly which ideas they would like to discuss and they will guide us to these most important ideas if they feel sure that the conversation assures the conservation of their integrity. It seems, therefore, that the issue which should be given most attention is the ongoing process we take part in when talking with people. This implies that we ask about all the conversations they have had and those they might have about the standstill situation in the future. They will point us toward the problem, which can be defined as something that one cannot leave and which one thinks has to be changed to something else.

MEANING-SYSTEM

Harlene Anderson and Harold Goolishian came up with some new points of view in 1985. We cite Lynn Hoffman, who at that time was also alert for "the new" (1985, pp. 386–387):

> The old epistemology implies that the system creates the problem. The new epistemology implies that problem creates the system. The problem is whatever the original distress consisted of plus whatever the distress on its merry way through the world has managed to stick to itself. You have to think of some kind of infernal tar baby or gingerbread man. The problem is the meaning system created by the distress and the treatment unit is everyone who is contributing to that meaning system. This includes the treating professional as soon as the client walks in the door. This position has been supported recently by Harlene Anderson and Harry Goolishian (Anderson, Goolishian, & Winderman, 1986) in their discussion of the problem-oriented system. Goolishian (personal communication, 1985) also makes a case against the prevailing emphasis on dividing therapy into individual, couple or family treatment. His reason is that as long as we use a framework based on social units, we fall into a linear mind-trap. If it is an organization, it can be dysfunctional. If it is dysfunctional, it contains pathology. If it contains pathology, we can go ahead and cure it. This brings us inevitably back to the old epistemology and the dichotomy between the person who fixes and the person who is being fixed.

These ideas have had a profound impact on our thinking. We see a problem-created system as an arena where many ones can be seen. Each of them has a tendency to stick to one description of the problem, having *one* corresponding explanation for it, and therefore, quite naturally also having *one* meaning for how it can be solved.

When each of those engaged holds meanings that are somewhat different from the meanings of the others, new meanings might emerge if the meanings are exchanged during conversation. If conversations do not exist, the meanings tend to stand still. Conversations most often stop if the meanings the various people hold are too different from each other. If prestige is also involved, people tend to hold on even harder to their meanings. In such situations people tend to listen to their own meaning about the others' meanings instead of listening to the others' meanings.

This understanding is one reason why we avoid expressing meanings. If we do, we easily become allied with someone already on the scene holding a similar meaning to ours, and inevitably become opposed to those who hold another and very different opinion.

Meanings-Systems as Organizations

Maturana (1978) and Varela (Maturana & Varela, 1987) emphasize the concept of organization as they use it. Maturana talks about organizations as composite units, being composed of two or more simple units. These units are such that the organization, combined in a whole seen by an observer, has some characteristics that give this organization its identity.

One can take a team working with systems as an example. The team is composed of four or five persons who come together to do systemic work. What they do together when they do systemic work characterizes the organization, the team.

The team might behave variously, sometimes one talking and the others listening, sometimes all talking; sometimes working very closely, sometimes less closely. These various forms of cooperation indicate various structures. Although the structures change, the core idea remains, namely, doing systemic work. Team members may be replaced by other persons,

but the organization remains if the new team still does systemic work.

In our "translation" to our daily use of language, we think of
organization as a grouping of two or more persons who have at
least one idea of common interest. As long as they hold this or
these ideas as a connecting interest, the organization prevails.
If the idea(s) disappear(s), the organization dissolves. In Anderson and Goolishian's terms (Anderson, Goolishian, Pulliam,
& Winderman, 1986; Anderson, Goolishian, & Winderman,
1986), a meaning-system can be seen as a group of people connected around the idea of doing something with(in) a certain
situation.

We in Tromsø like to look at that organization through certain lenses: What are the various sub-entities of this organization in terms of persons being able to talk to each other? In
other words, how are the various sub-units composed in terms
of people being able to exchange various ideas about the problem and the stuck system they created?

We have the feeling that many therapists want to make a
conversation with a group of people who are not able to exchange ideas at that certain point in time. So one of the questions we find very important to deal with is, "Who can talk to
whom about this issue in which way at this point in time?"
That does not mean that we cannot talk with all of them. It
just means that we should discuss with those who are engaged
around the problem which groupings we should meet with at
which time about which issue.

*Multiversa means that one and the same phenomenon, e.g., a
problem, can be described and understood in many different
ways.* The constructivistic idea that every person creates her/
his version of a situation is of great help when we meet with a
stuck system (Bateson, 1972, 1978, 1979; Maturana, 1978; Maturana & Varela, 1987; Segal, 1986; von Foerster, 1979; von
Glasersfeld, 1988). All versions are neither right nor wrong.
Our task is as much as possible to engage in a dialogue in order
to understand how the various persons came to create their
descriptions and their explanations. Thereafter, we invite them
to a dialogue to discuss whether there might be other not-yet-

seen descriptions and maybe even other not-yet-thought-of explanations. In a way, we invite them to join us in a flow of exchanges about the ideas, acknowledging that there is always something not seen and something not yet thought of in the processes of life.

In other words, there are always many other distinctions to draw in addition to those already drawn. The most helpful tools for us in drawing new distinctions are the questions not yet asked. The appropriate unusual questions are our best contributions to the stuck system.

People finding themselves standing still in what they define themselves as problematic situations are used to asking themselves the same questions over and over again. When we contribute to the process of creating new understandings of the defined problem, besides asking unusual questions in our conversation with them, how can we also create the possibility that each of them will start to ask new questions? In other words, how can we create the possibility for a person we speak to so that s/he starts to ask him/herself new questions?

THE REFLECTING TEAM

At this time our understanding is that the structure of the reflecting team offers the possibility for those who consult us, as they listen to the team, to ask themselves new questions, thereby drawing new distinctions.

The standstill system, whether it is one or more person(s), e.g., a family plus the helping system, is interviewed by one of us. All these persons belong to the interviewing system. The reflecting team is often behind a one-way screen and it is most often composed of three persons. A one-way screen is not necessary and the number of team members is not always three. These variations will be mentioned later.

The interviewing system is regarded as an autonomous system that defines by itself what should be talked about and in what way this should be done. The listening, reflecting team never instructs what the interviewing system shall talk about or how its members shall talk.

Each member of the reflecting team listens quietly to the conversation. The members do not talk to each other but each of them talks to him/herself in a questioning manner. They ask themselves: How can the situation or the issue(s) the system presents be described in addition to the presented description? How can the situation or the issue be explained in addition to the presented explanation(s)?

After a while, the team members offer their ideas if the interviewing-system wants them to do so. The team members then talk to each other about their ideas and questions about the presented issue(s), with the members of the interview system listening to them. In other words, each team member gives his/her version of the defined problematic issues. If the various versions are not too different, they will serve as mutual perspectives for each other, and the two or more various versions will tend to create more new versions as the team members talk to each other in a questioning manner.

Maybe even more important is that this procedure gives the members of the interviewing system (the standstill system plus the interviewer) a possibility to have an inner dialogue as they listen to the versions the team presents. After the team has finished its reflections, the members of the interviewing system talk to each other about the ideas they had while listening to the reflections. In a way they have a conversation about the reflecting team's conversation about the interviewing system's first conversation.

For the most part the interviewer asks questions and avoids giving opinions or advice. The team also only gives speculative reflections to underline that each team member can only have his/her subjective version of the whole and that, according to the basic thinking, there does not exist any objective or final version.

In this way, we see ourselves to be congruent with Maturana's saying that instructive interaction is impossible. We can only offer a chance for a transitional structural coupling of mutual interest, and the exchanges of ideas that follow. And we like to emphasize the importance of *mutual interest*.

Curiosity arises around the questions of drawing distinctions, e.g.: What would the conversation be if all the available but not used questions had been asked? What would be seen then? And which explanations could be constructed based on all these other not-seen descriptions?

I find myself more and more curious by thinking of the content of all the alternative conversations we could have had.

Replay of videotapes offers some possibility of dealing with those questions. At least we can figure out what all the unused questions might have been. We often replay videotapes of sessions and stop at one of the questions the interviewer has asked. Then we discuss which other questions we might have asked. It is not difficult to propose ten or fifteen or even twenty other possible questions. We also stop at openings not used and discuss which question we might have asked from these openings.

We can only be helpful contributors if the talk stirs our curiosity. As elsewhere in life, curiosity is a major contributor to evolution.

3

GUIDELINES FOR PRACTICE

Tom Andersen

These guidelines might be regarded as a sort of scaffold, as they can be set many ways and are transitional. They represent experiences gathered over time, and they have been helpful when appropriately unusual for those with whom we talked.

The most important part of the conversation resolves around the question, "How can the standstill system and we make a meaningful conversation together?"

Within the framework of that question, we basically talk about the various conversations that have been going on around the problem so far, and discuss which other conversations might be helpful in the future, with which person(s), which issue(s), in which way(s), at what time?

"We," representing the latest professionals on the scene, may be either one or two or three or four. Some of us prefer to be just one, asking the already existing professional(s) in the standstill system to join in a team. Some of us prefer that two or more of us become a team that meets the standstill ones.

WHAT WE CAN OFFER WHEN WE ARE A TEAM OF TWO OR MORE

There is usually one member of the problem-created system that connects with us, often a professional. The connection may be made by phone or by letter.

If it comes by phone one might start a conversation with this person about which persons are regarded as important persons at this time to be present at the first meeting to discuss the issue that is presented on the phone. If the caller is a professional, s/he is also invited to come to the first meeting. If that is difficult to arrange, the person is asked if we can stay in touch with her/him for information or further discussion.

If the connection is by letter, one might respond in writing, "Sometimes more than one person is engaged in dealing with issues like that which you have mentioned in your letter. In such instances it often seems helpful that we get to know as much as possible about the experiences and understandings these engaged people have of these issues. Since we do not know the circumstances around these issues, we want to ask whether there are particular persons who might contribute to our understanding. If there is somebody who could do so, they might come to the first meeting if they find that appropriate. If you are interested yourself, please feel welcome to be part of the meeting. If you cannot come, I hope we can be in touch with you if something comes up in the meeting(s) that we would like to inform you about or discuss with you." The idea is to raise the possibility that as many members of the problem-created process as possible will attend the meetings.

THE FIRST MEETING WHEN WE ARE A TEAM OF TWO OR MORE

If there are any professionals attending the meeting, we talk with them beforehand, explaining that we certainly want to have them inform us about their work with the system. We ask them to determine whether they want to give that information to us before we meet their client(s) or to give it with the clients listening. We say that we prefer the latter, but the professional(s) should choose the way with which they feel comfortable. They should at least not do anything that feels uncomfortable to them. The professional(s) are also given the option of sitting behind the one-way screen, either as member(s) of the reflecting team or as observer(s) sitting behind the team, just to watch and listen.

We have determined beforehand who will be the interviewer. The interviewer and one other person from the team meet with the standstill system (including the professional(s)) in the interview room, with the rest of the team waiting in another room. The nonprofessional members of the system are told the possible settings: only talking with one (the interviewer) or with two persons (the interviewer plus one other of us), or with the interviewer plus a team. They are also told the position the professional(s) has(have) preferred to take in the session. If a team is present, they are told that the team members will sit behind a one-way-screen. If there are more of us than the interviewer, they are told that once in a while the team might have a discussion about the talk the interviewer has had with the standstill system.

They are given the explanation that all persons who follow a conversation either as participants or as listeners often come up with ideas about what is discussed. Such ideas are often of value to talk about because they have proved to have a positive impact on the dialogue about the presented problem. Therefore, the team members will speak about their ideas openly, with everybody present listening.

If the nonprofessionals are uncertain about what they prefer, we leave them alone to discuss the options they are offered, and let them choose the format with which they feel comfortable.

After their decision upon the format, we introduce our wish to videotape the session, hereby also following their decisions. If there are students who want to follow the conversation, we then ask a final introductory question about that, and they determine whether it is permitted.

We do not hesitate to express what we believe will contribute the most to the conversation, e.g., the presence of the team. If they want to have a team participating, the team always comes into the room and all the team members shake hands with the members of the standstill system.

Before the start of the session we also often dim the light in the interviewing room and light up the observation room after the team members are seated, so that the standstill system knows where and how the team members sit.

WHAT WE CAN OFFER IN THE FIRST MEETING WHEN WE ARE ONLY ONE

In this case one of us goes to the local professional's office. We do so if the professional has agreed to be part of the meeting. The professional is told that we certainly want to be informed about the work so far. She/he is asked to decide whether that should be done before we meet with the client(s) or whether the information can be given with the client(s) listening. We say that we prefer the latter procedure but always follow what the local professional prefers.

We then say that only one of us will be the interviewer with the other one as a listening observer of the interview. That is explained as based on our experience that two interviewers most probably make two interviews, which can be hard for the attending client(s) to follow.

The local person determines what s/he wants to be, either the interviewer or the observer. The local professional most often prefers the latter.

Then we introduce the idea of stopping once in a while to discuss the conversation with the client(s) in a listening position. The local person is told to participate in that discussion only to the extent s/he feels comfortable. If s/he accepts the idea of being part of the reflecting team, we say that our experiences have told us that, in order to let the client(s) have the opportunity of being in a listening position, we should concentrate on looking into each other's eyes when we make our reflections. We say that if we look at the client(s) and thereby include them analogically in our conversation, we deprive them of the possibility of being in the listening position or, in other words, having the possibility of seeing the discussed issues from a distance.

If the local professional accepts these procedures, everything is explained again to the client(s) before they determine whether they accept it or prefer another format.

THE MAIN QUESTIONS

From the beginning of the session the interviewer and the rest of the team have some particular questions in mind:

What is the present ones' interest for this meeting? Who had the idea of this meeting first? With whom did this person talk about the idea first? With whom second? Who was then informed about it? Who liked the idea? Who was reserved? Did anyone resent it? Who among those present liked the idea the most? Who is most reserved? If the person who suggested this meeting had not done so, would anyone else have done it? And who?

For us the idea behind these questions is to get acquainted with the person(s) who is (are) most reserved about this meeting. They could be regarded as the conservers of the system. They should be given much attention during the meeting, because most probably they will be those who first give signs if the issue being discussed or the way the meeting is being conducted becomes too unusual. A glance at them every now and then to read facial expressions or a question about whether this is the appropriate time and setting for the discussion of *this* issue will give an answer to that. Who can talk to whom about which issue here and now? What are the issues the present ones want to talk about? What are the permitted formats for these talks? Should all be present? Should someone talk and someone listen? Should someone be behind the screen for a while, thereafter in front of the screen with others behind the screen? Should someone have another place as some others talk here?

All the questions above relate to the establishment of this conversation in *this* meeting with us. Both the interviewer and the members of the reflecting team wrestle with these questions.

Who Is Going To Be Asked about What, and Who Will Be Listening?

There are no firm rules but one idea is to first ask about the history of the idea of coming here if professional(s) are present.

The person who was most in favor of this meeting may later be asked the other main question, "How would you like to use this meeting?" or, "Which issue(s) would you like to discuss in this meeting?"

Everybody is given the opportunity to express commitment to the meeting and also to voice which issue(s) he/she would like to discuss. The further conduct of the session will correspond to this opening talk.

It might be that a particular family member has wanted a new consultant to be part of a conversation about some specific topics. In such case it might be the best to let the attending professional(s) have a listening position for a while before s/he (they) is (are) engaged in a dialogue with the interviewer.

On the other hand, it might happen that the professional(s) wanted the meeting the most. Two examples illustrate this: a consultant (a "specialist") to a standstill system consisting of a family plus a local consultee wanted an additional consultant to join. The "original" consultant had the idea of asking for another consultant. The consultee eagerly agreed. The family agreed politely. The consultant wanted to discuss certain concerns he had about the family. The consultee wanted to talk about some other concerns about the family that she had. The family would not have asked for any additional professional by themselves, and the family had no particular issue to discuss. In this case the new interviewer talked with the consultant and consultee about their concerns with the family listening. Every now and then the family members were invited to comment, which they did very little.

In another case a team asked for a consultation, clearly expressing their fears about recent happenings of unpleasant violence in a family that they thought might recur. During that meeting the consultant interviewed the team about the team's perspectives of the family's perspectives with the family in a listening position all the time. After the consultant had finished his interview, one of the team members turned to the family members and asked them whether they had any comments about what they had heard.

The Issues To Be Discussed

Everyone present is given the opportunity to say which issue(s) s/he would like to talk about. The interviewer talks with each of those who elicit an issue in a sequence and at a length that s/he feels fit the system's own ranking order.

Then it might be suitable to ask the present ones which format will best fit the discussion of the various issues. If the interviewer her- or himself is uncertain about the format, s/he may ask the reflecting team to convey its ideas of the various possibilities. The interviewer's cues for asking about such reflections can be that the flow of the conversation becomes too little to make a meaningful talk, e.g., when too few words and ideas are exchanged, or too much, as it is the case when several persons talk simultaneously in a quarrel. This might end in a shift to another format, e.g., splitting the group in subgroups etc.

By the way, it is important to bear in mind the questions about the format every time a new issue is brought up: "Who is prepared to talk to whom about this issue now?"

From Word to Word

Those who consult us are usually very well prepared for what they want to use the meeting for before we meet them. The first few sentences they come up with are most often composed of highly important information.

The interviewer is waiting for a pause in the system's stream of talking for his/her question, and as s/he waits s/he listens carefully to what is said. Something of what is said will become particularly meaningful in the interviewer's mind. Boscolo, Cecchin, Hoffman, and Penn call such utterances "openings" (1987, pp. 253–254):

> An opening is an expression of the meaning system in a family. It can occur in many forms: as an idea, a word cue, a theme, or a piece of analogic behavior. Whatever its form, it acts like an indentation, or an "opening," into the way a particular family

organizes its pattern of thinking, its behaviors, and the combination of meanings they collectively represent. For example, a father may say: "My daughter is too independent." The idea of independence is an opening; it is a word that is heavily invested with meaning for this family; and though a complaint is usually directed to a problem person, the opening has hidden distributions throughout the entire system.

I prefer to regard such openings as invitations for continuing the dialogue. One such opening becomes the basis for the next question.

Since we have to wait and see what the last sequence of talking contains, we can never know the paths the dialogue will take. We can only go from word to word.

The Observing System Chooses the Direction of the Dialogue

Those we talk with most often present many openings from the moment they start to answer one of our questions until they pause. They actually invite us to participate in more than just one new path of the talk. The interviewer chooses only one invitation at a time. What s/he chooses is his/her choice. Why s/he makes just these choices is impossible to answer completely. We prefer to believe that our choices are guided by our intuition about which opening will best serve the ensuing dialogue.

We hold it as an important rule to not follow an opening the interviewer her/himself experiences as unpleasant. The reader will hopefully remember from what has been said before that the interviewer, as well as all the other members of the team, represents organizations which must be given the possibility of conserving themselves.

The opening to choose may be the one that arouses some kind of curiosity. Cecchin says that such curiosity is very different from neutrality (1987, p. 406):

> In order to avoid the trap of oversimplifying the idea of neutrality, I propose that we describe neutrality as the creation of a

state of curiosity in the mind of a therapist. Curiosity leads to exploration and invention of alternative views and moves, and different moves and views breed curiosity. In this recursive fashion, neutrality and curiosity contextualize one another in a commitment to evolving differences, with a concomitant nonattachment to any particular position.

Issues that are felt to be unpleasant tend to restrain the curiosity, sometimes very greatly.

The Questions That Create More and Hopefully New Openings

These are the appropriately unusual questions. The response of the receivers of questions is the only indication we have of whether our questions are too usual, appropriately unusual, or too unusual. In order to "diagnose" our own questions we have to be sensitive to the responses of those we talk with. The too usual ones do not create any tension in those we speak to. The appropriately unusual ones do and that can be detected as some kind of shift in the person's activity, e.g., from easy thinking to hard thinking, a shift of the body from one position to another, from looking very at ease to a bit more uneasy, etc. – and all this occurs without any reduction in the flow of exchanges in the dialogue.

Too unusual questions also result in shifts in the person's activity, but these shifts are limitations of the person's openness for perturbations (our questions), e.g., they listen less attentively, become distant and uninterested, their answers are shorter and fewer, the activity of the bending muscles of the body increases and can be seen (e.g., a wrinkling face, arms being crossed over the chest, restrained breathing). If our senses are open for it, we can experience a reduction in the flow of the conversation. If we notice neither all the responding signs of the too unusual that are expressed nor the decrease in the flow of the conversation, we might notice that we ourselves are in a state of pushing: the less they receive our questions, the harder we push on them. This state of pushing can be noticed by our becoming more and more speedy, with a corresponding increased tension in our bodies. Therefore, we also have to be sensitive to our own state during the conversation.

Unusual Questions

There are many unusual questions one might ask at an opening. There is never only one question. Which question one chooses will certainly influence the direction of the discussion, too. The following is an attempt to offer ideas about a repertory of unusual questions from which one might choose.

The questions relate to descriptions of the activities around the presented issues, to the explanations of these activities and to what one can imagine if some(thing) of the activities shift. The three types of questions might be regarded as belonging to three different levels of the same phenomenon (Blount, 1985, pp. 150–151):

> We discuss epistemology, the rules for what counts as a fact and how facts are ordered into meaningful ideas, when we are discussing the organisation of the clinical services in an agency, because in systemic thought these are different perspectives on the same phenomena. Epistemology is the study of the ordering of premises in a particular setting. Agency structure is the organisation of behaviours or communication patterns in a setting. These are the same phenomena in any given instance. At any particular moment, the form of the act of communication and the form of what is being communicated cannot be separated. "Pattern of behaviour" is the concept used by an observer who is watching the pathways along which communication is travelling, i.e. the people who are communicating. "Premise of interaction" is the concept used by an observer watching the difference or information which is travelling along these pathways.

The shift from one type of question to another, which the interviewer does when and how her/his intuition tells her/him to do so, involves dividing descriptions from explanations and vice versa. People who stand still in a problematic situation easily confuse these two levels in their talking.

All questions are based on the crucial idea that people do not relate to the problematic issue "out there" but to their understanding of the problematic issue. A consequence of this crucial sentence is that we can neither describe nor explain the issue but can only describe their descriptions and explanations and give tentative explanations to our descriptions (of their descriptions and explanations). So one asks: "What did *you* see?" "What did *you* experience?" "What was *your* perception?" "What was *your* understanding?" etc., instead of asking questions like, "What is it?" "How is it?" In other words, people act in the problematic situation in accordance with their understanding of the problem.

Questions of Descriptions

It is essential to ask questions that produce double descriptions. Double descriptions give perspective to a phenomenon. Such questions comprise all variations of differences; they contain such words as:

— *in comparison to:*
   "How is it now compared to then?" (difference over time/ change) "Who liked it the most?"/"Who was most concerned?" (describing the phenomenon as part of a relationship) "Meeting with which grandchildren makes grandfather most happy?" (comparing relationships) "Who did what?"/"What helped the most?" (comparisons of attempted solutions), etc.
— *in relation to:*
   "What were the circumstances?"/"Who has been involved?"/"Who (of the present ones) has not been involved?" etc.
— *different from:*
   "When did it start?"/"When did it become worse?"/"When did it become less?" (different before and after a particular point of time), etc.

The reader's attention should be alert to the questions proposed by Mara Selvini Palazzoli et al. (1980), Peggy Penn (1982, 1985), and Karl Tomm (1987a,b, 1988).* These articles particularly describe circular questions. These questions will not be described here but only commented on. A whole issue of the Dulwich Centre Newsletter is devoted to articles on questions and questionings; the authors are Eve Lipchik (1988), Michael White (1988) and Laurie MacKinnon (1988).

An interviewer might think about this process as if s/he is asking the client: "Imagine that you have made a film of the problematic situation which contains all persons' movements and talks and ideas and feelings, etc. Pretend that you rewind the film and play it forward again in slow motion. When you do so, please tell me what you see and hear."

Sometimes questions about differences might be too unusual for those who receive them and, therefore, provoking. In such instances one just slows down and waits to ask them at a more appropriate time.

Sometimes people respond to questions about differences by pointing out and underlining the similarities of their various meanings. In such cases, if people heavily reject questions

---

*Our questions do not have the openly declared inventive or changing intentions Karl Tomm mentions. For me inventive and changing intentions seem to be in correspondence with instructive interaction, which according to Maturana we do not believe is possible (Tomm, 1987a, p. 6):

> This decision-making process is implied but not adequately accounted for in the three interviewing guidelines that the Milan associates originally described. Hence the appropriateness of delineating a fourth to guide therapists in making these choices. Strategizing may be defined as the therapist's (or team's) cognitive activity in evaluating the effects of past actions, constructing new plans of action, anticipating the possible consequences of various alternatives, and deciding how to proceed at any particular moment in order to maximize therapeutic utility. As an interviewing guideline, it entails the therapists' intentional choices about what they should do or should not do in order to guide the evolving therapeutic system toward the goal of therapeutic change. In labeling this guideline, I chose the root term "strategy" to emphasize that therapists adopt a stance with a definitive commitment toward achieving some therapeutic goal. The gerund form, -ing, was chosen to emphasize its active nature; that is, it is an active process of maintaining a network of cognitive operations that result in decisions for action.

about differences, one might ask about the tendency to be similar. "Has it always been like that?" "How come?" "Did it emerge
by itself?" "On purpose?" "By tradition?" etc. "Has it ever happened that anyone saw something a bit differently?" "If such
will occur in the future, who might that be?" etc., etc. But if
such questions are also too different, we ask about the issues
without eliciting differences, knowing that if we follow what
they feel comfortable with, there will be a time for questions of
differences.

Questions About Explanations

When differences are elicited, one might ask, "How can that
be explained?" "How can that be understood?" "How come it
happened at that point in time?" Unanswered questions about
explanations may be very good questions in the sense that they
create a wondering curiosity and a search for an answer.

After a change (a difference over time) has been described in
formulating the question about explanation, one might think,
"Which difference made that difference?"

When one deals with the history and notices that there are
leaps from the better to the worse and also jumps from the
worse to the better, one might think, "Which difference made
the difference to the worse, or, correspondingly, better?"

By the way, talking with a group of people, e.g., a family, it
seems that it is easier to speculate on questions about, "Which
difference(s) made the difference(s) to the better?" than on questions about the differences that made a difference to the worse.
Working with the latter rather negatively connoted question,
one easily turns on people's "defenses" and they close us off
from the conversation in order to conserve their integrity.

Questions About the Various
Conversations

Double or multiple descriptions are extremely helpful ways
out of a difficult situation. These come about through the exchanges of ideas of descriptions. When such flow of exchanges

halts, the problem arises. Questions about past, present, and possibly future conversations are therefore significant, e.g., questions like these:

"Who has talked to whom about which issue in which way?"

"What are the various meanings of the issue(s) and what are the meaning(s) of the solutions to the problem?"

"To what extent are the meanings negotiable?"

"Who are at present able to talk to each other about this issue(s)?"

"Who not?" "How can that be explained?"

ALTERNATIVE DESCRIPTIONS
AND EXPLANATIONS

"Future-questions" have been described by Peggy Penn (1985, p. 300):

According to the Milan associates, future questions break the pervasive rules that govern communication in the family—i.e., the rules for who is allowed to say what. Since the future is often indicated but not "set," no one is bound by formal contextual rules, and a different pattern may be imagined. For example, if you ask a family member a hypothetical question regarding future events, because the event is only now being considered, the system is free to create a new map. Then the communication of these new ideas about the future becomes important information introduced back into the present "time" of the system. They include fantasies, wishes, opinions, hopes, etc., all a part of the ongoing system and now unexpectedly called into play as part of the family's expressed interactions. In fact, repeated hypothetical questioning of an outcome—if this or that event obtained—gives the family a sense of their own potential to imagine new solutions. At that moment I would say the family are in the process of feedforward. In considering how things could turn out *if*, you are addressing a basic descriptor of the system: its capacity to evolve. It is that much harder for the system to restabilize when its evolutionary potential is evoked. The question is how (through what therapeutic mechanism) can one leave contextbound experiences and move ahead to new organizations.

An act is linked to a premise: the appropriate, the possible, the interesting, the unavoidable, the ought-to-be, etc. A change of the act or the acts connected to the act may challenge its premise and even change it.

"I noticed that you did the things in that sequence. If you change the sequence such or such, what would happen?" (Introducing and testing the possibility of change)

"I noticed that it has been done by him/her all the time. If s/he had to leave for a while, who would do it instead?"/"If you did it that way instead of this way, which problems might be raised?" (Introducing dilemmas: that another attempted solution creates another problem)

"If someone starts to talk about it, who would it be?" "You mentioned a certain dilemma, might there be other(s) to discuss it with?" "Would that be a friend or a relative or a previous close one who now is dead?"* "When would that happen?" "What would it be most natural to start to talk about?" "How should it be initiated: to write, to call, to go to the graveyard?" etc.

If we notice in the story people tell us that someone is deceased, we ask (as probably all of us will do) whether they still miss the person. If they do, we might ask whether the person is still somehow around. If the person is, we might ask how they communicate with the person. Then we might introduce the idea of making a conversation with the deceased one in order to find new ideas about the dilemma they are in (introducing the idea that other conversations might also be of value belongs to the cover-question, "Who might talk to whom about this issue in order to search for more descriptions and explanations?").

As with questions about differences, hypothetical questions

---

*A presentation by Arlene Katz inspired us to work out such questions about possible conversations with the dead. She let us see glimpses of a videotaped session when she visited us in North Norway in 1986: A young woman and her mother had physical ailments. The mother was the only survivor of a holocaust family, and her daughter the only person she now had in life. During the talks with Arlene the young lady had the idea of traveling to Poland to visit her grandmother's grave to talk to her. She did and brought with her a little bit of the soil of the grave, which she and her mother buried in the American soil. This event had a strong beneficial effect on the two women's physical health and also on their relationship.

might also be so provoking that they do not serve as helpful perturbations. The best thing to do is to wait and try again later when those who talk feel sure that the dialogue will not threaten their integrity.

If hypothetical questions about the future are constantly rejected, one might discuss the space for a self-determined versus a pre-determined future. "To what extent is it predetermined? Totally, or is there a small opening for something to be determined by you?" "Is it predetermined by destiny, a force, etc.?" "Will it be like that forever?" "If that changes, when will it mostly likely occur?" "If it will not occur who is most confident with that?" "Who will take the longest before accepting it?" etc.

LISTENING POSITIONS

A person in a listening position only participates in the inner dialogue. Circular questioning as it was implemented by the Milan team has a very powerful impact on the inner talk of that person to whom the question is connected, who actually is in a listening position. We arrange listening positions through the various versions of the reflecting team. The listening position could just as well be called a reflecting position.

Various Formats of the Reflecting Team

The team can be composed of one (the interviewer only) to four or even five (the interviewer plus three to four team members) people. That part of the team that listens to the interview-system's talk and thereafter talks with the interviewer-system listening to them is called the reflecting team.

If the interviewer is alone, s/he talks freely out in the air about her/his speculative ideas every now and then. If there is only one person in addition to the interviewer, this person most often sits in the interview room, but sometimes behind a one-way screen. When reflections are discussed in this format, the interviewer and the other person do that together.

The reflecting team composed of two or more, working either in the interview room or behind the screen, maintains one important practical guideline: the team members look into each others' faces when they talk, and they do *not* look at the members of the standstill system. If one were to look at them, one would invite them analogically to take part in the reflecting discussion. That would move them out of the advantageous listening-at-a-distance position.

If there is more than one person in addition to the interviewer, these people most often sit behind a screen, but they may sit inside the interview room. Sometimes, when there is a screen, the two groups shift rooms when the reflecting team talks. If there are practical facilities with double sets of microphones and loudspeakers, the two groups remain in their rooms and dim the light in the interview room and lighten the room where the team sits. The sound-transferring is correspondingly switched.

There is, as the reader hopefully understands, no single way of organizing a reflecting team. There are many ways to form it, depending on practical circumstances and the participants' wishes and preferences. Just to avoid misunderstanding it has to be made clear that the interviewer is always in the same room as the standstill system.

The Listening Reflecting Team

The interviewer conducts the talk totally independent of the other team members. This means that the reflecting team never interrupts to propose questions or advice.

Each team member just listens. If the team members sit behind the screen, they do not discuss the interview. The only talking that happens is when one member asks another what was said in the interview because s/he has not heard it. The idea behind not discussing is that a discussion behind the screen easily limits the team members' attention to only one idea or only some few ideas. When the team members do not talk to each other they will probably come up with more ideas and these ideas will probably be different ideas.

When the team members listen they collect in their minds the various openings as they emerge through either words or analogical expressions. One might say that they particularly select that opening which seems to be of great significance. If another opening emerges that seems even more important, one may let the first one go and start to elaborate on the new one. There are no rules about how a team member should work on an opening when s/he is in the listening position.

Basically I follow the same guidelines as the interviewer, "How can the mentioned issue be described? How can it be explained? What would happen if something else had been attempted? Are there any issues under discussion that at a first glance seem unrelated yet after a closer look are somewhat related? Is there anything expressed analogically that underlines something that is spoken? Are there analogical expressions in the sessions which are unrelated to and different from that which is spoken? Might these expressions be reflected on by the team or would such reflections be something that someone in the standstill system is not ready for?"

I often find myself asking about the characteristics of the talk's form and about those of the talk's contents. Is it the form of many monologues or of dialogues? Is there a stream of many ideas or of only a few? When the actual reflections are delivered one might think of this, "Should they be given in a monologue's form or as part of an exchanging dialogue? Should one stick strictly to just one certain idea or offer many ideas? Is the talk of the standstill system more intellectual and 'cool' or a bit more artistic or 'flowery'?" That might lead the reflections to be more straight forward in the first case and a bit more in the direction of metaphor and images in the latter. What is the speed of the talk?

THE SHIFT

There are two ways to shift positions: The interviewer may ask for the reflecting team's ideas, or the team members may let it be known that they have ideas available. It might also be a good idea to offer the standstill system the chance to initiate a break by requesting the team's reflections.

The interview system is regarded as totally autonomous in terms of the issues they discuss and how they discuss them.

If the team has ideas, they are introduced this way: If anyone on the team has an idea s/he believes might be useful to the interview system, this person says so to the other team members and asks whether it is time to announce this or whether the team should wait. If they agree that the time has come (only rarely do the others reject the idea of announcing because they usually think the proposer has a good reason to suggest the announcing), the person with the idea knocks at the door to the interview room and says to the interviewer, "We have some ideas that might be of some value for your conversation here. If you would like to have them, please let us know when that will be convenient."

The interviewer and those s/he talks to then decide whether they want to listen to the ideas and eventually when. It has never happened that the ideas have not been reflected on, but it has happened that the interviewer has waited many minutes before the team was called. In such instances the team may reflect on other openings than those they originally thought of, as new openings have emerged in the interim.

THE REFLECTIONS

If the reflections are given inside the room where the standstill system sits, the interviewer usually announces the shift, saying that the team will talk now. "You can sit back and listen to that conversation if you want, or think of something else if you want. This arrangement allows you to listen to and see what you yourself have been talking about from a more distant position." We have found this clear statement of the boundary to be useful.

Each member of the reflecting team bears in mind all the time that there are many versions of the issues that have been discussed, and that each member has his/her own version, which is different from the other ones. This calls for being a bit uncertain when one speaks, "I am not sure . . . , maybe . . . , one could think of . . . ," etc. Additionally, we use the word-pair both-and, "*both* this can be seen *and* this," "*both* this can be thought of *and* this," "*in addition* to what they saw I saw this . . . ," "I heard some strong explanations, maybe the following explanation could be *added to* what have been the explanations so far . . . ," etc.

The context of the reflections is what has gone on verbally and analogically in the interview room. We carefully omit from our reflections that which was shown during the interview that the person herself/himself seems to prefer not to have mentioned, e.g., a man might struggle in order to cover up his anger, or another cannot help showing a behavior of excluding someone but does not want that to be seen.

Our reflections often find the form of a dialogue and we put a lot of unanswered questions into them. We comment to each other and ask each other whether the others think of more or of something else.

There are very few rules to follow. The rules we have are all about what we shall *not do*: We shall not reflect on something that belongs to another context than the conversation of the interview system, and we must not give negative connotations.

As indicated above, we find it useful for the team to start to elicit the various members' most important idea or impression or issue, etc. Then we start to talk about the idea or the impression or the issue. When we first started to work this way we often found ourselves giving monologues. Over time we have turned to much more conversations among the team members, speculative conversations. One asks the others a question; they answer by raising more questions. If we understand that the standstill system wants advice and that it would be too unusual if we did not give any, we might discuss how another system in a similar situation tried to solve the problem. But we emphasize that a possible attempt to do the same should be stopped if it turns out to not help *this* system.

When those we meet talk in monologues, sometimes the team does the same; when those we meet are more towards the artistic side, we sometimes offer a metaphor.

The team very often speculates about which conversations might be helpful for the various issues. An issue is often talked about in terms of a dilemma, e.g., a family was very tolerant and understanding of other people's demands. "How was it for the various family members to stretch themselves so much?" "Might it be sometimes under certain conditions that someone did stretch him- or herself too much?" "If such situations occurred who could the persons discuss that dilemma with?"

The work of the Dublin group (Nollaig Byrne, Imelda McCarthy and Philip Kearney) has inspired us greatly. In their paper on incest, they define the incest situation as having created several dilemmas for many persons, e.g., should one disclose or deny? Blame or protect? Punish or support? Treat or punish? Define anybody as good and another as bad? Propose a hospital stay or a prison stay or a stay in a monastery? Self-punishment or punishment from men or God? Quiet atonement or open repentance? Etc. (McCarthy & Byrne, 1988).

We wonder to what extent we may reflectingly present the feelings that emerge in us when we listen to the standstill system's story. Most probably such feelings have two contexts: the dialogue we listen to and something from our own lives. For us how we shall handle such feelings is an open question. One family met with us because a teenager ran away; she was also a shoplifter. She was a daughter from the mother's first marriage. The mother had remarried and during the last three years had had two new babies. The stepfather seemed more attentive to his own two children than to the stepdaughter. One of the team members, feeling that the teenager had been excluded from the new family, talked about how he thought the girl might feel. When he reached the words, "Maybe she feels she is excluded," he had difficulty continuing. The feelings in the team member were so strong that he had to take several breaks to be able to finish. The family was stunned, and the runaway and shoplifting disappeared overnight.

The reflecting team (RT) usually talks between five and ten minutes, sometimes more. They are never interrupted by the interviewing system unless the reflections become such that those who listen cannot take it anymore. It happens very seldom, for us only twice. Once a small boy in a rather big remarriage-family became restless and very sad when the team talked about the family's long journey and wondered whether everybody had found a safe position within the new family system. His sadness and restlessness behind the screen were understood by the interviewer, who stayed with the family. The interviewer asked the family members whether they felt that they had heard enough. As they said yes, the interviewer knocked at the door and informed the RT that the family had heard enough.

THE INTERVIEW SYSTEM TALKS ABOUT THE REFLECTING TEAM'S TALK

When the reflecting team has finished its talk, the positions are reversed, with the interviewing system back to talking and the reflecting team back to listening. The interviewer starts the discussion with an open question, "Is there anything from what you have heard you would like to comment on, talk more about, etc.?"

Every person who does not talk spontaneously is given the chance to talk, since the question is put to each of them. When a person elicits an idea or more ideas, the interviewer asks about these ideas, following the same guidelines as before. After all who want to comment have given their ideas and discussed them (if they have any), the interviewer might her-/himself present for discussion the idea or ideas s/he came up with while listening to the team.

THE NUMBER OF SHIFTS

Usually we shift once or twice, unless it happens that the dialogue in the interview system is so rich, with so many new ideas, that reflections from the team seem redundant and therefore are not offered. Sometimes there might be more than two shifts; four is the most for us.

There is no rule that says shifts must occur. Both systems can offer or ask for ideas at any point in time.

Our rule is that the interview system shall always have the last word of a meeting.

THE FINAL PART OF THE MEETING

The future of the relationships of the present system, i.e., the interview system plus the team, is discussed in the final part of the meeting.

Do members of the standstill system already know whether they want to meet us again or not? If they know, do they know when that might be? Do they know who might come next time? Or would they prefer to think it over and call if and when they want another meeting?

In this passage of the dialogue we might discuss whether there were others to meet with instead of the team or someone in addition to the team.

One thing we have noticed since starting to discuss a possible future relationship this way is that we have the impression that people tend to need us less than we believed.

FOLLOW-UPS

Our wishes to follow up are stronger than our corresponding acts. When we suggest a follow-up it is said to be for our interest in knowing how they actually decided to handle their situation. When they come back some of the most interesting questions are about what they remember the most from our meeting(s). We ask those questions because we believe that what they remember the most has the most significance for them.

WHAT CONTRIBUTES THE MOST TO OUR FAILURES?

When we fail that can be readily felt, in that the standstill system has a decreasing interest in participating in the ongoing dialogue. In such instances we discuss immediately after the session, "How come?" If possible, reviewing videotapes can be very helpful in working with this question.

So far we can usually relate our failures to two themes. One is that we have not discussed thoroughly enough with the professional part of the standstill system which format the session should have. An example may clarify: A hospital ward we consulted for the first time met with us for only half an hour to discuss the format of the session before the family came. During the session with the family present we became aware that the routines on the ward (e.g., decision-making that seldom included the patient or his family) were in strong contrast to the more open and equal-participation-for-all style of our team. In hindsight we understood that we should have spent one meeting only with the ward staff to become acquainted with their mode of thinking and practicing, so that we would not be too unusual for them when we met with the family.

The other contribution to failure is that we do not discuss enough (or even forget to discuss) with the emotionally engaged (nonprofessional) part of the standstill system (family, friends, neighbors, etc.) the history of the idea of coming and becoming connected to us. It has happened that we have talked with someone all through the session without understanding that he had neither asked for nor was very interested in talking with us, even though a referring person was interested.

SOME FEW IDEAS ON PRESENTING

I have noticed that some persons in an audience who ask questions within a frame of "first-order cybernetics" have difficulties in receiving my answers, which belong to a "second-order cybernetics" frame. Therefore, it has been of some help for an audience to contrast the major ideas that characterize "first" and "second-order cybernetics" (Table).

After such an overview is posted on the wall, it seems to bring some relief to say that we all are constantly moving in our thinking back and forth between the left and the right side. It is easier to be on the right side when we have some distance on the issue in question, e.g., when we are "calm" in relation to it. On the other hand, it seems more natural to be on the left side when we are very eager in dealing with an issue or emotionally disturbed by it, e.g., angry or sad or fearful.

One does not have to be either on the left side or on the right

TABLE

First-order cybernetics	Second-order cybernetics
The "thing" (e.g., a disease) is seen as something in itself	The "thing" (e.g., a disease) is seen as part of and related to a shifting context.
A professional works with (treats) the "thing" (e.g., a disease)	A professional works with the person's understanding of the "thing" (e.g., a disease)
A person discovers the "thing" (e.g., a disease) as it is. The "thing" has only one version.	A person creates an understanding what the "thing" is, which is just one of many possible versions.
A personal change can be directed from outside; therefore, it is predictable.	A personal change evolves spontaneously from inside and one can never know what it will be or how it will be or when it will happen.

side. It is helpful to know where one is when one makes distinctions—in other words, to know where one's thinking is when one asks questions. If someone in an audience raises a question which belongs to the left side, one can say that an answer belonging to the right side might be confusing. Therefore, it might be of help to discuss the epistemological basis of the question before answering it. This should also apply to our own thinking.

Harold Goolishian reminds us all the time that " . . . you cannot not have a theory. But, remember that you must not fall so much in love with it that you have to carve it on a stone!" Such reminders help us to constantly revisit our own thinking. Maybe the shifting throughout our practice, from talking to listening positions, back and forth, also helps us revisit our thinking.

There is something in my article on "The Reflecting Team"

(1987) that deserves to be revised. I refer to page 424, the last sentence under the headline. Warnings: "The team must remain positive, discrete, respectful, sensitive, imaginative and creatively free."

On the one hand, this sounds like a command; on the other hand, it sounds as if the persons in the team have to be like that, i.e., to carry these qualities as parts of their persons. I think it would sound better this way: "If the time and the territory make it possible, one may try to bring a question or remark that is a bit unusual. So much unusual that it represents a surprise. Not necessarily a sweet surprise. But so much a surprise that the persons are given a possibility to be moved to another position and from there leave out of and/or add something to the descriptions they had before. When our right hand gives the surprising questions, it would be good if the left hand were open to receive and feel the person's reactings to what we uttered."

LET COME AND LET GO

The reader has come to the end of our guidelines, and soon s/he will let this part of the book go. This gives us an opportunity to deal with the words "let go" and "let come."

As Maturana says, life is constantly moving. The characteristic of the living is that it shifts all the time; life comes by itself. The moving life exists there, to let come, also with dialogues and the shifting descriptions and explanations they bring. The (shifting) dialogues exist as parts of the moving life. One does not have to make dialogues. Dialogues are already there to let come.

We included an interview with Aadel Bülow-Hansen in the book we wrote about her physiotherapy. In the middle of the interview she said: "I have to demonstrate something before you leave." One hour later, when I got up to leave not remembering what she had said, she said: "Don't go, I said I would demonstrate something. . . . Put one of your hands on my throat and one hand on my stomach. Now I will bite my jaws firmly. Notice that the breathing of my stomach stops. . . . No-

tice now. . . . I let the tension of my tongue and the jaw go. . . . "
She laughed and said, "When I let go the tension of my tongue
and the bite, my stomach started to breathe again."

She continued, "Over the years I have noticed that many
have difficulties with letting the breathing come by itself. It is
as if they want to control it. There is something strange with
letting the breathing come by itself. That seems to take a lot of
courage" (Øvreberg & Andersen, 1986, p. 10).

PART II

---

*Dialogues About
the Dialogues*

4

MIKE AND VARIOUS
DEFINITIONS OF A PROBLEM

Tom Andersen

Mike called and asked for a consultation. He is a general practitioner who works and lives so far away that we usually meet only now and then. Mike is strong and solid. Maybe this has contributed to his long sojourn in the area where he has been for twelve years now.

I cannot stop admiring him because his area is way out in the island-covered sea where sometimes the storms come and sweep everything away. Other doctors had been there working for a while, mostly a short while until a storm came and swept them back to the safe life of a city.

Mike stays.

He wanted to inform me about the patient, a woman in the middle of her fifties, before I met her. The woman had been a strong vital person, one others leaned on, always available and helpful, a surplus of energy. A cancer and the following operation four years ago had struck her to the ground.

"I cannot understand the change," Mike said, "and it is hard for me to accept the situation as it is now. She does nothing."

"She must be very depressed," he said, "she is lying down all day long. And she has much pain. I wonder and sometimes I believe that her depression is rooted in anxiety, and sometimes I think she is scared. I have not found the right route but I have been thinking that some way of having her air her fear of dying might help her."

"And," he said raising his voice and his neck, "according to my ideals one shall keep going as long as one can."

Time to give in shall not be until there is no way out. Accordingly, one definition in the system is that her protesting against a dark destiny is too weak.

The woman came together with her husband.

Both entered the room silently and slowly with bowed heads. Mike and she were seated side by side, with her husband on the other side of her.

The meeting started softly. The talk found a very slow pace. Mike had had the idea for this meeting. The couple had agreed to the idea without questioning it. Most probably they would never have asked for a session with a psychiatrist if Mike had not had the idea, they said. And a long pause filled the room.

She sat looking out in the air up to the right. Her eyes searched around all the time without finding something to rest on. Her wrinkles around the nose and between the eyes were deep but they did not move.

His face was bent a bit down as his eyes fixed on a certain point in the floor three feet in the front of him.

I trembled through my explanation that maybe Mike or I would come up with ideas as we listened to the conversation – ideas that might be of value for the conversation itself. Sometimes it helps to listen to a discussion that others do.

They nodded in agreement – but no words.

I wondered whether they understood what I tried to explain. People usually do not protest, particularly not out here where man's best protection is to obey the tough forces of nature.

A new long pause which she broke: "I have so much pain in my belly and in my back. I cannot do anything anymore. The time passes so slowly. I am of no use anymore . . . I don't know when I can be set free from here."

Then she continued her story, which I assumed she had told many times before. First, four years ago, being told that the cancer had gone far. So, operation and radiation. Then one year later, abdominal pain again, which everybody thought of as the cancer coming back but it had not, as the hospital concluded. Two more similar attacks of pain brought her back to the hospital, but no sign of relapse had been found.

Her slightly fainting voice and her eyes still searching for something somewhere told me that her fears for the returning cancer must have been tremendous – a bit more fear each of the four times.

And it was conveyed that it had been as if she were given back life every time they had not found any trace of the cancer, a gift that was harder and harder to receive each time. It takes a lot of energy to start to believe in life when it is given back four times.

She had pain. All the time, she said.

And she had had problems with the water for the last three years. She could not control it. She used diapers but was not sure whether such remedy could prevent the smell of urine. To be safe she lay all day. This helped to diminish the leakage.

She had not been in touch of mentioning any fear of dying so far. Her definition of the problem seemed to be related to the physical complaints.

I thought that the discussion should also comprise Mike's definitions; therefore, I commented on one of her first statements about not knowing when she could be set free from here.

I felt that she understood where my path could lead her and she immediately cut off by saying that she couldn't know whether she was going to live with her complaints in twenty or thirty years. Her taking me away from this issue I tried to touch made me ask whether she had been talking to someone else who might have suggested something to be done.

Well, her daughter and daughter-in-law had thought there must be something. Her husband interrupted, saying that three years is a long period. Maybe something has been invented lately which had not been available three years ago.

She eagerly watched Mike when her husband talked.

I suggested that Mike and I talk for a while with the couple listening to us.

Mike did not know that the three women had been discussing what might be done with the water problem. "I thought,"

Mike said, "that the diapers had solved that problem but now I understand they have not."

After a short pause, he continued, "I must admit that most of the time I have been wondering what kind of thoughts might follow such a disease? Are there unspoken thoughts? If there are concerns, and even worries that could and maybe even should be brought out into the open?"

"Yes," I said, "sometimes that might be very relieving. Sometimes it even diminishes pain. On the other hand, if she wants to talk about her inner thoughts with someone, who could this person be?" Both of the couple listened carefully but without watching us. "I wondered," I continued, "if any of those who surround her are ready to participate in such a talk? Would it be wise to encourage such talk if not all around are ready for it?"

When we turned to the couple, she said that all her life would improve if the water leakage diminished. That would make her more active in all respects. "And," she said, "that will help me endure the pains."

The disease is said to be over. All examinations indicate that, she said. Not the smallest word had touched on the anxiety around a returning cancer.

Turning back to Mike, I said that my contributions at this meeting did not seem to be very great. It seems to me, I said, that the main issues to be addressed were best taken care of in the relationship between them, Mike and her.

Mike agreed without hesitation.

What a gift, I thought on my way home, for people to have a doctor who is able to rethink his definitions of a problem and even change them.

I visited the area one year later and Mike wanted me to meet with him and the couple again.

The couple was strikingly more satisfied compared with the last time. Their clothes had brighter colors and their eyes were here and not somewhere else.

This time Mike told me the story with the couple listening.

The meeting with the surgeons in order to repair her leakage had been without success. It was hard to take, but she did not regret the attempt.

Shortly after this disappointing message she had had a bad backache that took her to the bed for two months. And while restricted to the bed she had pneumonia. The times were duller than ever.

"I took it very seriously," Mike said, "and sent her to the hospital to have her back examined with a special x-ray method."

Fortunately nothing serious was found, and she was back on her feet shortly. "But," Mike sighed, "that was not the end of it. Shortly after she recovered from her backache, she had a bleeding ulcer that took her back to the hospital once more."

I expressed my surprise that they looked so well after such a tough time.

The couple confirmed Mike's story.

They could not explain how everything had turned to the better. And best of all they said, they did not think of the "disease" anymore—it is behind.

"Then," I said, "maybe the time has come to look forward? Are there any plans for the immediate future?"

The atmosphere in the room shifted. She said smilingly that they were going to their hut for Easter holidays—a summit for the family every year.

"Is there more to look forward to," I wondered, "to look forward to with joy?"

He said: "No, I cannot say . . . one has many strange ideas in the back of the head . . . "

"What is that?"

"Oh, that is sort of ideas one has to drop . . . "

"What do you have in the back of your head that you have to drop?"

"That is a kind of secret."

"Is that something your wife knows?"

"Maybe she knows but that is just a wish dream."

"Is it an unachieveable wish dream?"

"I think so."

"What does your wife think about it?"

"I am not sure."

Since my curiosity had been raised it would be exciting to know about it and I asked her: "Do you know what he is thinking of?"

No, she didn't know.

I said to him that it would be exciting to know.

He could not resist smiling and said: "I want a bigger boat."

"How big is the boat you have now?"

"Fourteen feet."

"How big would you like it?"

"As big as to be able to sleep on board."

He said with eagerness that, if he had a bigger boat, he would be able to go to an area filled with small islands divided by narrow sounds. He is in love with that place, not only with the land but also with the beautiful houses there.

If he had a bigger boat he would take his wife with him.

Both husband and wife laughed.

Then the conversation turned back to the old days when they and the kids together went with the small boat to the islands not far away to fish and to go ashore to cook the fish. This contributed so much to their togetherness in former days.

She would love to go with him again.

She thought that would even strengthen her in all respects. We all laughed and talked about what had to be done to have the dream fulfilled.

Money. More money than they had. He would not buy a new boat; rather he would rebuild an old one.

"Do you think you will start making plans?"

"I don't dare think of it."

Mike had been slightly moving on his chair the last few minutes; he wanted to talk.

We turned to each other and he said: "It all sounds very optimistic to me. It might indicate that the optimism has returned . . . at least to some extent . . . that they are looking to the future is encouraging. I don't know whether this is inappropriate but looking back on the last year there has been something happening that has made me uncertain."

Now his head is slightly bowed as he says: "When she was in deep pain with her backache without any of us knowing what the explanations could be, I could not resist asking her whether she was afraid that 'the disease' had returned."

"You mean the original cancer four years ago," I asked.

"Yes," Mike said, "and my question is whether I should have asked that question or not."

I suggested that the answer should come from her and her husband.

Her mild eyes comforted Mike's face, and even though words were not necessary, she said that those thoughts were behind them now – forever.

In the short pause of relief for everybody there was an opportunity to repeat that maybe the time has come to look forward and to wonder with Mike whether this meeting had reached its own end. Leaving the room, I could not resist asking the husband whether he would send me a postcard from one of the small islands he loved if he went there in his own boat one day.

"Sure," he laughed.

"Sure," she laughed.

5

TALKING ABOUT LEAVING, BEING LEFT, AND BEING LEFT OUT: FOUR REFLECTING CONVERSATIONS

Tom Andersen

This chapter comprises transcripts and summaries from a workshop in September 1988. It demonstrates one of many ways to organize reflecting positions. Present are members of the system that defined themselves to be a standstill system, plus a group that watched the whole session on a video-circuit-loop.

When I am a consultant I try to contribute in such a way to a conversation or to several conversations at the same meeting that new ideas might emerge about who, what, how (in what way), and when. Who might talk to whom about what issue in what way at which point of time? Sometimes it might be helpful to concentrate on new ideas about who, sometimes on what, sometimes on how and sometimes on when, sometimes on more than only one of these four aspects, sometimes even on all of the four.

The invitors who were part of the standstill system work at a "special" school for children who for different reasons are not able to take part in ordinary schools.* Part of the philosophy behind the work at the school is connected to tendencies in the society to which the school belongs. In this country the principles of public services have reached so far that, e.g., all preschool children can stay in kindergartens. This rather strong development of support from the society, however, seems to have had a certain "side-effect" on some parents, such that society through its services has taken over some of the parents' tasks in relation to their children. This school wants to do something with this deparentizing tendency by encouraging the parents to take over their parenthood again.

At the start of the workshop, there was an overview of the composition of the standstill system. A teenage girl, Britha, was a pupil at the school. Two family therapists met with the mother, Dora, Britha, and Ilya, the five years younger sister. Since Britha attended classes at the school, people from the school were also present at the workshop. A team, consisting of three members plus their supervisor who had consulted the family therapists, was also in attendance.

We gave an overview of the four organizations making up the bigger organization of the workshop day: the family plus the school (teaching staff and the therapists) plus consulting team plus myself as a new additional consultant.

We took about one hour to discuss the format of the meeting. Which of the four groups should participate in which way? Who should interview? Should there be an observing team? Should there be a reflecting team? Several possibilities were raised.

As we thought about the history of the system present on the workshop day, some ideas about format emerged. The history of that system was that the two therapists wanted a consultation in addition to the supervision they already had. They had asked the other staff members at the school about this idea. They complied. The consulting team, being the next to be asked, also wanted to meet. The family, being the third to be

*The school was Framnässkolan, Stockholm. All names in the system have been changed.

asked, was also willing to come. The professionals agreed to
wait to give any information about the family and the therapeutic work until the family was present.

All the professionals, who took part in this discussion, wanted all conversations to take place "in the open," i.e., all members
of the system could be present all the time, either as talkers or
listeners. They wanted me to be the interviewer. The final format agreed upon by all was this: I should start to talk to the
two therapists and to the one teacher-assistant from the school
with the consulting team and the family watching the conversation from behind the one-way screen. Thereafter I should talk
to the consulting team, with the family and the therapists and
teacher-assistant watching from behind the screen. Then I
should talk to the family, with the teacher-assistant and the
therapists and the consulting team watching from behind the
mirror. And finally the professionals of the standstill system
(the therapists, the teacher-assistant and the consulting team)
should come into the room and talk, with the family and myself
listening to that conversation from behind the screen.

The staff of the school met with the mother, Dora, and her
younger daughter, Ilya, to explain the format and to find out
whether they felt comfortable with this format. They liked it.

Britha did not show up.

THE FIRST CONVERSATION

I, the interviewer, who had no more knowledge of the system
than what has been told so far in this chapter, talk first to the
two therapists (Ted and Tim) and the teacher-assistant (Teresa)
with the family (Dora and Ilya) and the consulting team watching from behind the screen.

At the school there is a family therapy unit and a teaching
unit. These two parts work separately. The teacher-assistant
had not participated in a family therapy session before. The
family therapists have been meeting with the family since
Britha came to the school six months ago. She has been there
on a daily basis and stays home at night.

For the most part they have met with the family every second week and during one period even weekly. Most often Britha has been present, but she is absent today. The consultation team has been working with them every now and then from the start of the therapy. Dora is divorced and the school has never met with her ex-husband (Britha's and Ilya's father).

My thinking before this conversation was: I should try to do my best to make my questions be connected to the relationship between the school and the family. I would certainly be open to wishes to deal with the relationships within the family system, but in doing so I would try to compare those relationships (within the family) with the relationships between family and school.

INT: (*to all*) What would you prefer to use this meeting for?

TED: Be given the opportunity to wonder . . .

INT: Excuse me?

TED: To speculate and get . . . and maybe broaden our perspectives . . . I must say I don't know whether what we do is fruitful or . . . I would like to know where we are going.

INT: You seem to raise two issues – the first is to wonder whether that what you do is of any use, and the second is to wonder where you are actually going?

TED: Yes.

INT: What have you actually done? And where are you going from here?

TED: Yes.

INT: What would the two of you (*turning to Tim and Teresa*) like to use this meeting for? Do you have any preferences?

TIM: Yes, I think what I would like . . . because I have thought of this, "I wonder whether this is my problem," since Dora says that she is pleased with us and these meetings and will continue them.

INT: I understand.

TIM: But I am also sitting with that speculation . . . I watch Britha every now and then at school . . . I think these meetings are very well . . . but I think . . . when I see Britha at school, I ask myself, "Are these meetings meaningful?"

INT: What do you see in school that makes you ask, "Does it help?" What happens at school . . . ?

TIM: I can see very little change in Britha. She frightens the adults. She acts out. I am not often at school, but when I see . . . and when her mother said she had to leave home for a period, then I wonder, are we of any use for the family? Are we of any help? I have started to wonder whether this is only my problem.

TED: (*interrupts*) That is where we are . . .

TIM: (*continues*) I am just more and more confused.

INT: So, Britha's mother says she likes to meet you?

TIM: Yeah. Yes, she likes it.

INT: She is satisfied?

TIM: Yes, she thinks this is a good school.

INT: But you are in doubt about whether these meetings help Britha?

TED and TIM: (*simultaneously*) Yes.

INT: Are you at any time in doubt that the meetings help Dora (*the mother*)?

(*Pause*)

INT: Do you doubt that?

(*Pause*)

TED: Well . . . (*Pause*)

TIM: The question is whether we help provide any change?

INT: OK. (*to Teresa*) Would you like to say something?

TERESA: Seen from a school perspective I feel Britha is hanging loosely in the air. As I understood Dora, there are plans for Britha to move from home. I have heard from the social services that this is determined. But nothing is determined with respect to when or where. To another institution or to another (private) home? So, from Britha's point of view it might feel meaningless to put any efforts in schoolwork. She has been pretty much absent from school lately. She is very shifting. Sometimes she works concentrated and well. Sometimes unbalanced and acting out. At such times she feels bad and she is very restless. And on such occasions it is hard for me to know how I shall work with her in school. I can understand that she does not attend school and has difficulties in putting herself into it, as she does not even know how long she shall stay.

INT: Yes.

TERESA: That is how I see it.

INT: You said that there are days she can function very well at school, even lately?

TERESA: Yes, she has certain days.

INT: And she can function less well . . .

TERESA: Yes.

INT: . . . if I understood you correctly?

TERESA: Yes.

INT: And you said everything is hanging loosely in the air . . .

TERESA: Yes.

INT: . . . because she is going to move but it is uncertain where she is moving and how?

TERESA: Yes.

INT: Who had the idea that she should move?

TERESA: (*Pause*) I understood there have been discussions between Britha and her mother during the last four months. Britha has sometimes agreed with the idea, sometimes not. The mother has decided she shall move.

INT: So this has been a discussion within the family?

TERESA: Yes.

INT: Did any others have an idea about it?

Further summarizing: If mother will, she will get help to find a place for Britha. Many people involved think Britha should live at an institution.

Mother wants Britha to move out. Britha herself is uncertain. Ilya, the little sister, does not want her to move. The

interviewer summarizes: There are two big questions: Is therapy of any use and where shall Britha stay?

What does Britha wish in her heart? One of the therapists
thinks partly she wants to move, partly she is very sad about
that solution.

Moving from home will also remove her from these meetings. They believe that Britha thinks that the school supports
mother's wish for Britha to move. It comes out, however, that
periodically mother also wants Britha to stay at home.

Who else can Britha discuss her dilemma with? She has nobody. A grandmother? No. An aunt? No, but she had a cousin
who herself lived at an institution and came to their home on
weekends. Who can mother discuss her dilemma with? A
girlfriend. In addition, the meetings here are most meaningful.
What in the meetings does the mother like the most? That the
team exists and is there; the discussions in themselves are not
the most important. And the team accepts Dora just the way
she is. Dora has no one other than her friend and the team to
talk with. She has not talked to her own mother or father. She is
very uncertain about whether that would help. Inviting Dora's
parents to the meetings has been considered, but the idea was
never pursued for reasons not very clearly understood.

How come, I ask, it is easier for Dora to talk with you than
to her parents? It has become a habit. There is a long history of
connections with professionals before us. Dora seems to have
had difficulties leaving her mother. So Dora might understand
her daughter's dilemma around leaving? Yes.

The therapists believed it would be difficult for Dora to go
back to her mother for advice. I ask, do you believe that Dora
believes that will always be difficult? They do.

If the relationship between Dora and her mother improved,
would that influence the relationship to the team? Most probably. How? In the strivings to find an answer a thought emerged
in the team: Dora's leaving her original home has never really
finished. So, she is still in the process of leaving? A surprised
"yes" indicates that this is a new idea.

The school-assistant says that she has never talked about
the relationship between Dora and her mother before.

This first conversation took thirty minutes.

THE SECOND CONVERSATION

A shift is suggested and the school-assistant and the two therapists go behind the screen to join Dora and Ilya while watching. The consulting team of four (three team members, Crystal, Christopher, and Christine, and the supervisor, Sue) comes in front of the screen to talk with me.

This was my preparation before this second conversation: I felt that what I could do best was to ask questions that were connected to the relationship between the consulting team and the family therapists. I thought that the team might also have ideas about the family and maybe they wanted to discuss that. But if that happened I would try to connect or even compare what was going on in the family to what was going on between the family therapists and in addition to that what was going on between the family therapists and their consulting team. But that should happen only if the consulting team seemed to feel comfortable with such questions.

INT: (*to all*) Please, choose yourself what you want to answer first of these two questions: Do you have any ideas about or any comments to what you just heard and do you have any particular wish concerning what you want to use this meeting for?

(The various persons in the room laugh and move slightly on their chairs.)

CRYSTAL: I feel that I am in the same position as the family therapists, wondering whether what we as consultants do helps . . . (*Pause*)

INT: Help in relation to what?

CRYSTAL: Both in the relation to the therapists and in the relation to the family.

INT: I see.

CRYSTAL: Are we of any use?

INT: Have the therapists themselves told you anything? (*Pause*) Or, in other words, what is your understanding of the therapists' perception of the help you try to provide?

CHRISTOPHER: It seems to me that the therapists' uneasiness about their feelings that nothing happens with the family was greater last week than today.

INT: You say uneasiness . . .

CHRISTOPHER: Uneasiness that nothing happens.

INT: When did you perceive that the uneasiness was not so big?

CHRISTOPHER: Today.

INT: Oh, . . . today!

CHRISTOPHER: They felt more uneasy last week. So did I, too. Which is related to the school. How it works at school.

INT: How Britha is doing at school?

CHRISTOPHER: Exactly. If she was doing without problems at school I would find it easy to sit here and talk with the family about whatever. But there is an uneasiness about Britha's doing at school. Do we do the right things here? My uneasiness has been greater than what I perceived was presented in the talk we just heard here today. Maybe that is only my uneasiness (*looks at the others in the team*) . . . ?

INT: Maybe I misunderstood the therapists, but my understanding was that the sign of whether the meetings with the family were good or not so good would be seen in Britha's performance at school? If the meetings were good that would correspond with Britha behaving well at school?

ALL THE TEAM: Yes.

INT: It seemed that the conversations with the family according to the therapists' point of view had the aim of making changes to the better at school?

ALL THE TEAM (*nodding*): Hmmmm.

INT: Might it happen that the conversations could be meaningful in other respects, in addition to their meaningfulness in relation to the school?

(*Long, long pause*)

CHRISTINE: As Christopher said, I have this feeling that I as a team member . . . have sort of lost the position of being at that distance that is necessary to help the therapists with new ideas. I have also had this uneasiness. I have been pulled into it, I have not been able to stay outside (*pause*) and that is why we wanted help today.

CRYSTAL: What I was thinking of when you (INT) asked the therapists . . . it seems that they are wondering about whether the conversations help Britha since she behaves as she does at school . . . you asked whether these conversations are good for Dora . . . And they did not really answer that question.

INT: If they had answered, what do you think they would have answered?

CRYSTAL: The idea came to my mind was that, "Is it such that the conversations might be good for mom and not for Britha? Do they have to be good for everybody? Do they have different wishes (from the school)?"

(*Long, long pause*)

INT: (*to all*) May I go back to my question: What are your perceptions about the therapists' perceptions of your contributions to them? Are they satisfied or are they dissatisfied?

SUE: With our contributions?

INT: Yes. (*Long pause*) If you were going to guess?

SUE: I think they feel like mom that they are rather pleased with the help we have given them even if they do not know whether they themselves were of any help so to speak. (*The others in the room move on their chairs and "hmmmm" their agreement.*) But we have worked hard . . . but what I am thinking of . . . when you ask like that . . . everybody strives hard . . . extremely hard . . . in order to help mom and the girl . . . because everybody has perceived the utmost sufferings between mom and the girl. Not only because she does not behave in school but also because the girl says she does not want to live . . . and expresses the suffering of not being able to help the girl to want to live . . . mom is striving, Ilya is striving, the

therapists are striving, we are striving. But I don't
know whether Britha and Dora are suffering less after
all these strivings? And I think of what we could hear
in the conversation [INT had with the therapists and
the school-assistant]. Dora describes that during the
sufferings mother feels close to the girl and that
makes me wonder whether there is anything in the
fights and the sufferings, which we perceive as difficult, which might make it difficult for us to see the
closeness the mother gets by the fights and the suffering. Do you understand?

INT: Yes.

SUE: I am thinking, maybe there is something in the
suffering Britha cannot let go because there is something good in it. And we are striving and striving but
maybe that is what they are not looking for?

ALL THE OTHERS: Hmmm (*in agreement*).

INT: So it might be understood in another way, so to
speak?

SUE: Yes.

INT: It is not necessarily only suffering but comprises
other aspects as well?

SUE: Yes.

CHRISTOPHER: They are very close. There is a lot of
contact.

SUE: There is a strong closeness between mom and the
two girls.

The following is a summary of the rest of the conversation:
There are some questions about what the therapists have understood of the form and content of the difficulties which have
existed between Dora and her mother and father. The difficulties seem to be somewhat similar to those between Dora and
Britha. The conversation then turns back to the already twice
raised question about what the therapists might find useful
and meaningful in their relationship to the consulting team.
The consultants and their supervisor believe that the fact that
they exist is the most important. That they are there. What
they talk about and all the new ideas are not the most impor-

tant, although such parts of the work are certainly important. That they exist makes the therapist feel less uneasy. Maybe not feeling so uneasy makes them less eager to make changes?

The interviewer suggests that there might be some similarities between Dora's feeling safer just knowing that the therapeutic meetings exist and the therapists feeling less uneasy knowing the consulting team exists. A new question is raised: Which problem or problems might emerge if you in the team told the team and they told the family, "We are here as long as necessary, until eventually others come to take our positions?" One said: We would have a problem since we want the team to make it without us, and the family to make it without the team. Another said: We would have a problem in not succeeding in changing Britha, by not producing effective ideas for her relationships at home and at school – we would feel it hard.

One said that one new idea had emerged. This was connected to the goal: "I feel the goal is the problem."

Another said that they might certainly remain behind the therapists, but that not having the notion of doing something meaningful would be felt as a problem.

Since these answers seemed to be somewhat firm opinions, I turned the conversation in a different direction by first mentioning that two goals seemed to stand out: to provide some kind of change to the better both in school and at home. Could other routes be found for a change to the better in school? Since the school-assistant had spoken about some days being good days for Britha and some less good, would it be an idea to work with the question: What are the contributions that make a school-day a good day for Britha? Which persons might be interesting to talk with in order to search for an answer to that?

A new shift is proposed.

This second conversation took eighteen minutes.

THE THIRD CONVERSATION

The consulting team goes behind the screen to join the listening position of the therapists and the school-assistant and the mother and Ilya come in to talk with me.

I had no particular plan before this third conversation – just to follow the mother and the daughter where they wanted to go. Maybe my way of making distinctions and asking questions would allow the already engaged professionals to see some new aspects of the family in addition to all that they had seen so far?

INT: *(to Ilya)* Are you tired?

DORA: Yes, Ilya is very tired.

INT: Was it hard to listen to?

DORA: Yes.

INT: What was the most hard to listen to?

DORA: *(sighing, long pause)* Well, *(pause)* it is like Britha escapes.

(Ilya moves on her chair.)

INT: That Britha escapes?

DORA: It seems that I am so much in the center. She is not participating. That was what I was thinking of.

INT: That she is not participating?

DORA: That makes pain.

INT: That makes pain?

DORA: It runs like a scarlet thread throughout: that she starts something, then quits, and I have to continue the job.

INT: You say that makes pain. Can you say something more?

DORA: She is not doing so well and she is not getting the help she needs. And she doesn't know what to do to get it either.

(Long, long pause)

INT: So, she might be absent because she needs more help or another help?

DORA: Hmmmm *(yes)*.

INT: And that hurts you?

DORA: Hmmmm *(yes)*. It has taken so many years.

INT: Where do you feel the pain? Where in your body can you feel it?

DORA: All over the body. The stomach.

INT: What helps to reduce the pain?

DORA: (*Answering soft and inaudible something about Britha being more pleased with what happens to her*)

INT: I wonder when you have the pain, what usually helps reduce the pain?

DORA: I don't exactly understand.

INT: You say that you feel pain in your stomach. I wonder what helps you to decrease the pain?

DORA: Actually nothing. It just continues.

INT: Just continues?

DORA: Yes, and then it passes away by itself.

INT: So you wait until it goes away?

DORA: Yes. (*Long pause*) For example, when there are fights there will be another feeling.

INT: A feeling to the better or to the worse?

(*Long pause*)

DORA: Both. Sometimes I feel I can control the fights and that makes me feel better.

INT: Who takes part in the fights?

DORA: Britha.

INT: You and Britha?

DORA: Yes.

INT: Sometimes the fights make the stomach feel less pain and sometimes more?

DORA: Yes. Sometimes I feel compelled to keep silent. That I cannot speak up. That I cannot talk to her. I want to talk to her but I feel I have to speak to her through other persons.

INT: In such situations do you feel that you come somewhat closer to each other?

DORA: Yes.

INT: If that pain became very strong and you had to express it somehow through affects, how do you think you would express it? Would you be angry or would you cry?

DORA: It would vary but most often I feel an urge to cry.

INT: To cry. If the pain became so strong that you had to cry, who would be available to comfort you? (*Long, long pause*) Who in your life would come . . .

DORA: (*interrupts*) That is not a question of comforting. That is a question of, who would be willing to comfort?

INT: Who would come and put an arm around you and say, "Just cry"?

DORA: (*interrupts*) Sometimes I wish that would be my mom.

INT: Is there any hope that that might happen one day?

DORA: I don't believe that will happen.

INT: You say you don't believe but is there any hope that it might happen?

DORA: No. Today I feel I have to comfort her.

INT: When did you stop hoping it might happen?

DORA: When I first realized, I was nineteen years old. There was no contact anymore.

INT: Do you think there will come a day when you start to hope again?

DORA: Yes, that is possible. That is not totally impossible.

INT: Do you have anybody to talk with about whether it is wise to hope or not wise to hope?

DORA: No.

INT: You have nobody to talk with?

(*Long, long, long pause*)

DORA: Just so.

(*Long, long, long pause*)

INT: It sounds sad. (*Long, long pause*) Do you want to say something, Ilya, in relation to all you have heard the others talked about?

ILYA: What did you say?

INT: Would you like to say anything about what you have heard?

ILYA: No.

INT: Was it boring?

ILYA: (*nodding "yes," pause*) I am tired.

DORA: She almost felt asleep when she listened.

INT: Oh, oh! (*All three of us laugh.*) I propose that we end this meeting. It might be interesting for the three of us to go behind the screen and let the others come here to talk if they want to make any exchanges. I am not sure that they want to talk but that is a possibility. What do you think?

DORA: That would be fine.

INT: They can choose to talk about just what they want to talk about. And we can choose to listen or (*smiling at Ilya*) sleep if we want.

ILYA: (*smiles*) Hmmmm (*yes*).

INT: Maybe you (*Ilya*) can walk in the garden if that is OK with your mother? Would that be OK with you, Dora, if she waits outside if she wants?

DORA: Yes. She seems to be very tired.

INT: (*to Ilya*) What would you like the most: go with us or go outdoors?

ILYA: I can stay here. I don't enjoy making any decision.

DORA: You can be with us and then go out if you change your mind.

The positions are shifted. This third conversation lasted eight and a half minutes.

THE FOURTH AND FINAL CONVERSATION

Dora, Ilya, and I go behind the screen to listen. Ilya was there for a short while, then she left the room and came back a couple of minutes later and stayed with us.

The therapists and the school-assistant and the consulting team talk in front of the screen. This group of seven starts talking pretty soon.

Christopher comments on what to his mind seems to be similar, namely the relationship between Britha and her mother (Dora) and that between Dora and her mother. From Christine's perspective it becomes clear that everything seems to be connected—what we (at this school) do and what they (in the family) do and what we all (school and family) do in common. And nothing of what happens has any value in itself since we cannot know what it might affect in the future.

Teresa has the impression that so much has been concentrated on how Britha is doing. At the same time, as we hear Dora
talking, Britha somehow disappears. Her feeling after this
meeting is that Britha is lonely. Christopher says that, on the
other hand, it seems clear that she has her mom, who, Crystal
says, carries a lot of responsibilities which she (Dora) feels she
cannot leave.

Ted does not know whether what is said now comes from
what was heard or from something that was thought of as he
listened, but the question is, "Do we talk with mom all the time,
also about Britha, instead of talking directly to Britha? Do we
leave Britha out?" Christine heard that (what Ted just spoke
about) as mom's perceptions of what happened.

Others now talk about the possibility that the many involved professionals, in mainly addressing the mother, might
have induced some kind of limitation in the possible talks between Britha and mother and Britha and the professionals.

Thereafter, Ted says that what flashed through his mind
were all our ambitions to do and to achieve. "I must start to
warn myself to do that, for example, in relation to the possibility that Dora may start to hope again. I must sit back and let
that happen when Dora and her mother find that suitable to
happen. I must avoid wanting to initiate it." Christine says,
"Dora needs comfort but there are not so many people there.
Britha is in the same position, she also needs comfort. On the
other hand, does her behavior become a barrier between her
wishes and what others might give?" "And grandmother needs
comfort," Ted says.

It seems to Sue that Britha represents a very important
aspect of Dora's life. It might look hard now, but maybe in the
long run it will be wonderful for Britha to know that she represents so much meaningfulness for her mother. Britha seems to
work hard, Christopher says, but does she feel it as hard or as
not so hard? Does the closeness and love that follow the fights
make her not feel it so hard? Teresa has no doubt that Britha
feels it hard. That is what can be understood by meeting Britha
at school. "But I am sure she strives hard to make everything
change to the better. That's what I see."

Christine feels, at least when speaking on her own behalf, that until now the meetings have been good for all in the family. But does that have to happen? It seems that the meetings have been most meaningful for Dora, and Britha is somewhat outside of all of it. If it is like that, maybe we should not overlook the possibility that something is reflected from the mother to Britha, even if we do not see the big effects.

Teresa wonders what can be done from now on after this experience (today)? "I might focus more on Britha at school. I feel she is lonely. Does she need more from the school? So far I myself have had limited contact with Britha. Mostly I have been in touch with the mother. Maybe I should be more in touch with Britha on an individual basis?" Christine asks whether Teresa wants to replace mom? She first says, "Yes," then: "No, not replace the mother, but I have kept a distance from Britha because of loyalty to the mother. What I have done has been to back and support the mother, and maybe in doing so I have left Britha out. In the first months of Britha's stay at the school the bad behavior happened at home, not at school. But lately that has changed so it happens more at school now."

Christopher wonders how long a parent is expected to give and give to a child. "Shall one give maximally the whole life through? May a moment come when it ought to stop? That has happened between us (the therapists and the consulting team). Sometimes you have wanted us to come back. How long shall it last like that? Dora has been giving the maximum of what she can all the time." Ted asks whether it is time to stop, "before we say so much that we become overloaded?"

Everybody agrees and the meeting is over. The last conversation lasted twelve minutes, so the consulting as a whole lasted one hour and ten minutes.

Only time can tell whether new ideas will emerge. Maybe there are some indications in the final, fourth, conversation. Are there some new whos, or some new whats, or some new hows, or some new whens appearing in this final conversation? The reader and I will most probably make different distinctions, so I wonder which ones the readers will make.

When the video-cassette arrived at my office four weeks

later, a small note was attached. Part of the note read: " . . . The most exciting is not on the tape. The process that followed, that between the school and the consulting team, which the consultation with you became part of, was what was most valuable. The content, all the sayings on the tape, are not of such significance."

Having my curiosity raised by that cryptic note, I wrote, asking them to tell me about that process. This is what they responded:

When we watched the tape, weeks after the consultation, we were struck by how little such a tape catches. It captures only small fragments of all the feelings that exist, both in the interview room and in the observing room. And the tape does not tell anything about the context in which the consultation took place.

For the family, particularly the mother, maybe the least important was what was said during the conversation. What mattered most was the new experience of sitting in the positions she was given — in a kind of meta-position to her own life situation and the problems connected to her daughter.

Eight professional helpers were directly involved in the treatment of her daughter, who herself was not there. Eight professionals who thought, talked, and speculated about them. The situation seemed to have a great impact on the mother, and maybe the meeting made the mother take the full step: to let her daughter be totally taken care of by the society. (The words and the conversations were not significant, after so many years of therapeutic conversations.)

So, by letting mother have the positions she had during the meeting, she handled in itself what we have tried to handle for a long while, namely clarifying that the mother and daughter needed official persons between them in order to be able to be connected. The consultation gave even us, the professionals, the chance to verbalize this. And according to the mother's response to the meeting, just that was the most important for her.

As her position changed in relation to us during the consultation, certainly our position changed in relation to her, and also to our work with her.

Actually, we ended up in a meta-position to our own way of

working. For the staff at the special school, which the consultation actually seemed to aim at, the consultation seemed helpful. It influenced the development at the school, which has gone on for a while, namely to find new ways to cooperate with the children and their families, apart from the idea that the children will only change if the parents change first.

All these "hang-around" hypotheses are interesting. First they (the hypotheses) open up new perspectives, make us, the professionals, less prejudiced, more nuanced (varied), more curious, and closer to those we meet. After some years they (the hypotheses) become constraining and make the whole boring. We should be able to make it without them (the hypotheses) the first years.

Would your current non-interest in hypotheses be possible without your first years with them? May we skip them as we train those who we are supposed to train? We must admit that we don't believe you have no hypotheses, or your own thoughts about what you hear, but we understand you don't bother with formulating them for yourself or others, since we believe you think other processes are more important.

6

AFTERWORDS: CONTINUING THE DIALOGUE

Arlene M. Katz

My colleagues and I were listening to the reactions of a couple* who had just heard our own reflections as part of a reflecting team consultation (Andersen, 1987). The husband, Richard, who moments before had been so despairing, began to smile which then expanded into laughter. He explained that he had been suddenly struck by the humor of it all:

> R: You tend to think you go through these vital shifts and changes when you're 16, 17, 18 and you sort of get it over with. And here we are, sitting in basically the same situation. The scope is a little wider . . . but you're just as baffled now as you were when you were a child.

The whole idea of *problem* became amusing to him, particularly as he heard it being talked about on a professional level, which "takes it down a peg or two":

---

*All names and other identifying characteristics of the family members mentioned and/or quoted in this chapter have been changed.

R: Let's not get uptight about it. You're aware of this but you don't necessarily see it all the time; the patterns that you're going through are pretty standard patterns, you're not the only one who has to deal with them.

We were struck by the spontaneous reactions of families to this process, particularly when they heard our own reflections on their conversation. Most people who seek help come expecting the experts to offer statements and judgments about them. We reasoned, what if we invited back those who had come for help originally and asked them to offer *their* statements and judgments and to engage in a mutual inquiry about the reflecting team?

We were aware of the limitations of any one description, which, though it may capture one aspect, cannot *be* what is described. "The only truth that will approach the absolute level is the truth which the thing itself might provide if we could come that close to it, which alas, we can never do" (Bateson & Bateson, 1987, p. 151). Rather than search out an absolute "truth," we would give each other the opportunity to *see* a new aspect, to acquire new information, neither theirs nor ours but something else, newly emerging. Here I am using *seeing* in a particular way: " . . . as seeing oneself through the eyes of the other. If it were otherwise, it would be blindness" (von Foerster, in Segal, 1986, p. 166).

If we were to only hold our own view or search for one particular answer, we would risk becoming blind to the information held by the client system. We need instead to position ourselves in such a way as to invite an exchange of perspectives that creates a mutually derived language. The reflecting team is one way to have a particular kind of conversation on purpose, a dialogue that invites comparison of differing viewpoints. The format (Andersen, 1987) provides enough time for both the client system and the team to listen and to participate. It is designed to give everybody concerned the opportunity to shift position on purpose, e.g., from listening to participating, from talking to listening, and back again. The reflecting team consultation is a variation in which a therapist requests a reflecting team to consult to ongoing clinical work. It begins with a discussion between the therapist and the interviewer in front of the client system. Next the clients are interviewed while the team listens. The clients then listen as the team reflects on their conversation, and finally, they are given the chance to react to these reflections. The comparison of these dual perspectives can promote a genuine double description.

> In principle, extra "depth" in some metaphoric sense is to be expected whenever the information for the two descriptions is differently collected or differently coded. (Bateson, 1980, p. 79)

The format of the reflecting team is designed to realize this Batesonian notion; as it invites one perspective then another it becomes a way to embrace the possibility of both. Each description becomes a point of comparison, an opportunity for new ideas, a different perspective on a problem. This subtle awareness of difference usually makes a difference of its own (Bateson, 1980). The focus is on tracking the evolution of ideas about a "problem" over time and in the present conversation with the interviewer, a co-evolutionary view rather than a more fixed problem focus. The interviewer can best orchestrate or create the context for conversations of this type by making room for multiple views, rather than trying to look for absolute truths (Anderson & Goolishian, 1988; Goolishian & Anderson, 1987; Hoffman, 1985, 1988). Otherwise, if we hold any one view to be the only correct one, we risk a monopoly of ideas and the eventual collapse of the conversation (Bråten, 1987).

We anticipated that the various people involved in these dialogues would create different kinds of description, which might be woven together in one narrative or might stand as a collage. To weave events from different time frames, people construct "nested narratives" demonstrating varying levels of coherence. These stories evolve in response to new ideas as they are re-told by different people, in different contexts, at different times (Gergen & Gergen, 1988).

Meaning is generated by this process of mutual story-telling and by the exchanges within self and between self and other. This quality of dialogical conversation has been described metaphorically as "a breathing exercise between people"; exhalation followed by inhalation; "let go" and "let come"; now listening, now talking (Andersen, 1987, personal communication). The metaphor itself becomes a way to collapse duality. As Koestler reminds us, both poets and scientists use metaphor to permit two previously unconnected frames of reference to intersect . . .

> The difference between them is the character of the "frames of reference," which in the first case are of a more abstract, in the second of a more sensuous nature. . . . (Koestler, 1975, p. 320).

STORIES

This chapter is devoted to the stories told by client systems in conversation with the author about their experiences with reflecting teams composed of Norwegian and American professionals. These were part of ongoing exchanges between Norwegian and American clinicians meeting together in reflecting team consultations to ongoing clinical work.* In these cases the *reflecting team* consultation was requested by the therapist who was already involved with the clients. The initial *reflecting team* meeting took place in the familiar surroundings of the referring professional: a physician's office, a private practice office, the office of a physical therapist, and a mental health center. The team met in the same room with the family or behind a one-way mirror. Three months later, a second *afterwords* meeting took place in which the author interviewed each couple with the referring professional present, following certain guiding questions (Andersen & Katz, 1987): You most probably remember you met with us and some Norwegians on

---

*I would like to thank the following colleagues who were involved with the clients in this chapter for their ideas and participation on the various teams: Tom Andersen, M.D., Anna-Margrete Flåm, Ph.D., Ted Chapman, M.D., Chantal D'Arleville, Barbara Perryclear, L.I.C.S.W., Marjorie Roberts, Ph.D., Lynn Caesar, Ph.D., and Doug Phillips, Ph.D.

(date); what are the impressions you now remember from the meeting? How did you react to listening to the team converse about the conversation you had with the interviewing therapist? What questions were you most occupied with before the meeting?

These questions were meant to open the conversation and to generate other questions that could be explored in depth as they evolved within each conversation. The intention was not to meet with the families to satisfy our own curiosity or to merely provide answers to our own questions (Andersen & Naess, 1986). It was necessary to hold our questions "in parentheses,"* and not to be too attached to any particular outcome. Rather, they would be guidelines to generate other perspectives or ideas, questions, or concerns in whatever direction the conversations might evolve. They were designed to continue the dialogue begun with the reflecting team.

This form of follow-up moves the clients' original issues into the new context of the afterwords interview – three months later. Though there may not be an explicit problem focus, each narrative reflects what is *currently* most important to the couple and the extent to which the couple continues to be occupied by their original concerns. The process by which the clients offered their present views created a perspective on the past and a fresh view of the present.

The afterwords interview provides a context; it is not a new research technique but rather the chronicle of a way of thinking.† The narratives form a collage of descriptions of the client systems and those of the author, a portrait of mutual inquiry. Excerpts from the afterwords interview are punctuated with the author's thoughts at that time and her reflections while writing the narratives. What follows are descriptions of de-

---

*See Mendez, Coddou, and Maturana (1986) for a more extended discussion of the importance of keeping "objectivity" in parenthesis.

†See Atkinson and Heath (1987), who discuss a model of research more akin to ethnography: " . . . the process we are suggesting is one in which researchers retrace the distinctions they have drawn in constructing any view of the data, so that the reader may do likewise. In a sense, the reader is taught the *process* of constructing a view" (p. 13).

scriptions, a story of stories to which the reader is invited to add his or her own ideas and questions.

In the text that follows, the initial consultation is the *reflecting team* interview; the followup meeting is the *afterwords* interview. "A" denotes the author and "I," a reflecting team interviewer. Unless otherwise indicated, the transcripts of the conversations are excerpted from the afterwords interview.

KALEIDOSCOPE

Reflecting Team Summary

We being with a glimpse of the conversation between the interviewer (I) and the therapist (T) in front of the couple and the team.

I: Are there any particular issues you want me to discuss?

T: Maybe the desire for closeness between John and his former family . . . and the distancing felt by his wife. I feel this is important because Claudia is going through a lot, and those important to her are . . . distancing from her. The other part is John wanting to relocate and Claudia feeling distanced by his desire to move closer to his family, so she feels isolated.

I: Might all these things be connected somehow? Have you been discussing it with them?

T: No, this is new . . . this is now.

This couple, John and Claudia, told a story of shifts and changes within themselves and with those to whom they feel most connected. For Claudia, it was a time of creative expansion and exploration of the new; for John, a time of focusing inward on himself, of stepping back and sorting out. His reconnection with past relationships had a profound impact on the present and posed questions about the future. For John, the death of a parent and the unexpected birth of a grandchild stirred up old feelings of homesickness, which became a prob-

lem. These shifts and changes created questions about relationships between fathers and sons, and about how the past may
inform or create new possibilities in the present and future. For
Claudia, questions opened around emotional expansion – is it
safe to be vulnerable or is it too big a risk for her and for the
relationship?

Afterwords

The afterwords conversation with John and Claudia became
a kaleidoscope of changed and changing perspectives; we begin
with the wife's picture of her experience of the reflecting team
in words and metaphor.

A: Could you describe the process as you experienced it
   of having us converse about your conversation in
   front of you?
C: The system is like a mirror where you look in and see
   what you see. If I look in the mirror and describe how
   I look, it would be a particular way; if my husband
   stood behind me and described how I looked, it would
   be something else. And if someone else stood behind
   me, it would be something else again. And they would
   all be true. I felt that was what the process was about.
A: It was like multiple mirrors in a way?
C: Right. It's like a tunnel; in order to grow or to expand
   at all, you need other feedback that says, "This is how
   I see you," and it's a part of your truth. And someone
   else saying, "This is how I see you" – but doing it in a
   way that you can hear it.
A: The image I had was like a kaleidoscope, with the
   different mirrors reflecting.
C: Right.

Both Claudia and her husband thought that the reflecting
team process was very powerful, but that certain conditions
were necessary for it to be successful. They agreed that it had
created a nonjudgmental atmosphere where there was a basic

level of trust. They were particularly impressed by the honesty of having professionals share their thoughts in front of them. They felt this generated a "request to be honest" on everyone's part, but they still felt reserved in certain ways, e.g., finding themselves in a slightly different setting, with new people. However, they sensed that if these meetings were to continue, they would gradually feel more comfortable.

Claudia had been particularly sensitized to the interviewer's concentration and the care that he took with what he said; ironically, at times this was mirrored by her own caution and made her feel more reserved. However, she did notice a difference as the team conversed—there was an openness to their exchanges that made for a more relaxed atmosphere.

She had come to the reflecting team with an agenda—to focus on the couple relationship. When she suddenly felt emotional in the interview, it was something unexpected and she hadn't been sure what to do with it. In the course of the interview, she became puzzled: should she stay attached to her own agenda or be open to whatever emerged? I wondered, would there be room for different ways for her agenda to be addressed? Since that time, she has become aware of other perspectives.

C: I feel that I got a lot out of the session, even though I came in with some kind of sense of what it was going to be and in the end . . . I didn't get that! But as I started processing it, I got everything I needed.

A: How do you explain that?

C: For me I believe you always get what you're going after in one way or the other. What happens is that you wear blinders. And you think it's going to be orange and because it comes in the form of blue, you don't see it because you're waiting for orange.

A: The sense I had is that you created more room in the conversation you were having with yourself. You started with orange and there was only room for one color; at some point, there was room for both orange and whatever color came in?

C: Right, [though] not within that time.

A: Not within the session itself?

C: Oh no. It took me a long time to process everything –
it was a lot!

The couple wanted to make a distinction between the process that had begun in the reflecting team itself and how it had evolved since then. John thought that the meeting had catalyzed or stimulated a process; his wife described how she had "rewritten the story of the interview many times" in the three months since the meeting.

I wondered, what had been the effect of these rewrites? The original problem that had organized her coming to the meeting was somehow released. She realized that during the initial (reflecting team) meeting, a piece of information had unexpectedly emerged that had given her a fresh perspective. Something shifted for her when the interviewer had asked, "What would happen if John left?" At that moment she experienced a profound sense of self or wholeness – a realization that she *could* make it on her own even if circumstances changed. With that, her focus shifted from the agenda *as she had anticipated it* to a sense of relief and of trusting herself. There was now room for both her own agenda about the couple and whatever other new ideas might emerge. She felt the "problem" was addressed but in a way that was different from what she had expected.

A Timed-release Capsule

As Claudia spoke I was reminded of how a "story" can change subtly with each telling, by different people or by one person over time. In the following dialogue, she describes how her story evolved – sometimes weaving in new experiences, then returning to glimpses of the interview to give her experiences a different kind of sense, from a new perspective:

A: Can you give a brief [description] of the different parts
of the processing you did?

C: It hit me on a lot of levels. The first week was all

superficial stuff, "I wish he would have done this," and, "well, if only he wouldn't have said that," and the next week I'd go to the next level and it's deeper.

A: Would you feel free to give me some sense of what the levels were?

C: It has to happen in your life; that's when the truths hit for me. During the session I was angry with John, his kids . . . his not moving in the direction *I* thought he should move in; *my* agenda, *my* timetable (*laughs*). He was not doing it!

Over a period of time, it's just feeling the truth of that. Then it's . . . dropping off some of the anger, not pushing so hard, not feeling frustrated that he hasn't jumped five feet because I measured the five-foot mark! And realizing that it's his own agenda.

And that, as I detach and pull back, all of a sudden he starts moving! And I'm going, wait a minute, I stopped pushing and he's moving! Then you start to feel the truth of your involvement and you start to feel the truth of those kinds of dynamics.

And then you look back at the session, and . . . then it all falls into place!

When she "let go" of her first agenda and shifted her position, she noticed new options and the irony that there was a shift in John's behavior as well. I was aware of how this experience in her life led to a new construction of what had happened in the session — another rewrite.

A: So you then described the session in a different way? There was a different story of the session.

C: Right, because all of a sudden a little kernel of the truth happened in your life.

You needed to feel your anger, you needed to feel that wish — that some other force would come in and save you from it; that you wouldn't have to do anything, that someone else would come in and make John do what you wanted him to do. But it was still

all *my* agenda. And it took a long time to process that
and to look at the session differently . . .

A: It was like a *timed-release capsule* or something?

C: Yes! Who gave it to me and when is it going to go off?

John's own descriptions were of a different quality; his
first reaction to the reflecting team was evoked by his fantasy
that,

J: Omigod, they're going to talk about us while we're sitting there. No wonder he's choosing his words carefully! You could have these visions of what doctors say
when you're not in the room, "Did you see that guy?"
Maybe they do, but you folks certainly didn't. So I
didn't feel violated at all in terms of your discussions.
I thought it was very nice. I'd rather be there.

John's ideas had also evolved over the last three months; his
style was to suddenly sense something that he hadn't been
aware of before—a blip on the radar screen that would signal a
shift in perspective. He had come to the reflecting team feeling
quite homesick for his children. As he described this to me
three months later, he suddenly changed his description and
made a distinction between how he felt homesick then and how
he feels now:

A: So the questions that came up from the meeting
stayed with you in certain ways?

J: I didn't realize how angry Claudia was about the whole
thing . . . I hadn't realized it until this evening . . . I
think what I got out of the session was that the homesickness wasn't really the issue. Maybe the realization
was that coming home in myself was what I needed to
do.

A: So the story at the beginning of the session was of
being homesick but then at some point, during the
session or afterward, it shifted and it was no longer an
issue . . .

J: It just suddenly dawns on me that that's not true. The *blip on the radar screen* says, you're not homesick. Homesick is a real different feeling.

A: How would you describe this as different from home-sick?

J: It's not the same feeling. Homesick is this aching in your chest, you just feel lonely or scared inside – tight across here, butterflies in your stomach; that's home-sick. And that wasn't the feeling I had – what flashed through my mind was a feeling of loss . . .

A: So that the meaning of the initial issue or agenda shifted in the course of –

J: Yeah – probably not in the course of the session, but between the session and now. . . . My hunch is that it definitely catalyzed or stimulated a process.

Claudia added her view that when a person goes into a situation like the reflecting team, something unexpected might well emerge:

C: I think whenever you go into a situation like the reflecting team – not that you're not nervous about it. . . . There has to be a willingness to face a truth that might come up that you've kept in your back pocket.

And maybe you know it's there but it hasn't been spoken and no one else knows about it yet, so you just prefer to keep it in the back pocket. In any situation like that, you risk that it's going to be pulled out and everyone is going to say, look what's been in her back pocket! And why is it there? And what's it doing there? And what does it mean for everyone else . . . ? That's the kind of thing you risk.

Claudia has raised some questions that will have special significance for the next couple. When secrets are revealed, do they open up new ways of looking at what may have been a problem, and is this likely to be experienced as a relief or add a burden? The next couple addressed these questions and dealt with the effect of new information that came to light after the reflecting team.

LOOKING FOR A HOME

In this narrative, we begin with a summary from the reflecting team consultation in order to set a context for the changes that followed.

Reflecting Team Summary

The couple, Laura and Michael, listened intently as their therapist described their work together. Woven throughout the story was the wife's longstanding search for a "home," first in herself and later for an actual home. In times of crisis or when Laura has felt particularly disconnected from her husband, she would again feel compelled to search for a new home.

Home was a strong metaphor for this couple. For Michael it meant being connected to himself on a deep level and feeling grounded, "that I had been away on a trip and was *back home . . .* just here, in me." In the reflecting team interview, the question of whether home was a house itself or the life inside of it was a profound one for Laura. She described that her grandmother's house evoked her image of "home"; she felt that grandmother was "still around" and continued to be an important source for advice, for wisdom, for friendship, for love. Her feeling of being at home was disrupted when her husband distanced in a particular way that she felt as "disappearing."

The couple was occupied by the effect of a breakdown Michael's father had some years earlier. Michael recognized in himself certain things that he had seen in his father; certain similarities stood out in bold relief and he feared them – becoming distant and withdrawn in ways that would disconnect him from those closest to him. At the same time, he also felt that the breakdown had created an opening to know his father somewhat better. The fear of being too similar to father was evoked as Michael described how it would be if he were to have a breakdown: his family would be completely alone even though he would still be there physically – in the same way as he had experienced with his father. Yet, if he *did* have a breakdown, he believed that he would eventually get closer to his family:

> I: How could that be explained? What kind of changes might implement that?
> M: I just think that if I fell completely apart, then I would want to get myself back together again. . . . After I put myself back together again, I would be stronger or more together.
> I: More grounded?
> M: More grown and more grounded.

And the reflections from the team included these ideas:

> T1: I wonder if there's a certain kind of space that would allow for Michael to be quiet without it seeming like he had gone away somewhere?
> T2: Be quiet without disappearing?

and,

> T2: I wonder, would it be necessary to go through such a big crisis as they fear or could that grounding be implemented otherwise?
> T1: I had that very similar thought.
> T2: Could there be another route to the same aim? I was wondering about that. They both certainly would like to have him in the home that his wife would like to have.
> T1: And he'd also be in his own house, his own home (inside himself), as well as being in her home.

Other reflections wove in ideas about how an atmosphere could be created to reflect the feeling of home, how a distinction could be made between Michael's wish to take personal time for himself and his actually disappearing, and whether some message might be left as a signal. We discussed whether conversation with others might offer new ideas, e.g., with the grand-mother, with the father, and between the sets of fathers and sons.

Directly following the reflections, Michael talked about how important it was for him to be allowed to just do nothing, some of the time. He agreed that there was an important distinction between having that space and disappearing. Laura also began to ask herself certain questions: Do I somehow contribute to Michael's disappearing? If I could trust that he was still con-nected to me, I wouldn't have to seek him out to make sure he's still there. Some new ideas emerged about her fears of his hav-ing a breakdown:

L: The fear that I have – I keep close tabs on him.

I: Which makes him close down?

L: Which may make him think he has too much to do or that he has to go away. I don't know. If I could trust that he's generally there, I wouldn't' have to keep such close tabs on him. It's not like I ever thought of this consciously before; I'm just thinking of it now.

I: Maybe you should allow yourself to think it over and don't push yourself to any kind of solution.

Afterwords

Looking back on the reflecting team, Laura recalled the agenda she was holding when she came to the meeting: impor-tant ideas that had to be addressed about their relationship, Michael's holding back, and the impact of his father's break-down. What had not been talked about represented a major part of the couple relationship, and she had been relying on her husband to bring up certain topics himself. She told us that, "not only were we talking around things but you could only talk around them as well because you only had the information that we gave."

Though she thought that what had been discussed was most helpful, she was still conscious of what had *not* been said. This narrowed her focus and attached her to a hoped-for outcome; when it eluded her she felt frustrated. However, there were times when this urgency allowed her to absorb new information, e.g., when she talked about her grandmother and *felt* that relationship again as she reflected back on it; she also had a *sense* of what it meant to look for a home.

Michael viewed the reflecting team "as an experiment . . . going with the flow of what was happening," and felt himself to be open to whatever might come up in that conversation. Laura interjected that by taking that stance he was holding "part of himself very secret." The difference in position – Michael open to what was happening and following the conversation as it unfolded – was felt by Laura as something that shut out the agenda that *she* was focusing on. Could there be room for both?

Michael's strongest impression of the reflecting team was of "a very kind and comfortable atmosphere for us to talk." When asked what in particular made for that comfort, he replied that it was partly that the conversation took place with a man, who seemed to generate an atmosphere of comfort. This allowed him to risk talking in an unthreatened manner about his father and about the impact of the father's breakdown on their relationship. He believed this to be a major underlying factor in his current marital crisis; being able to talk about it now was an important opportunity.

Michael had been particularly intrigued by listening to the team reflecting on the conversation they had had with the interviewer. He continued, "It was really interesting to get feedback . . . to hear what you had to say about what we were saying . . . that was really helpful. . . . It was a unique way to do it."

He had never before been in a situation where the professionals shared their views in front of him and it seemed more balanced. He had always felt the pressure to come up with everything himself. He was genuinely moved, saying, "Sometimes I feel I just want to hear, 'well, what do *you* think about it' – I'm sick of coming up with everything. . . . So to me it was a relief; all right, 'What *do you* think about it?' Because you never hear that!"

Their therapist was curious about any reactions the couple had to her talking with the interviewer about them while they listened. She asked, "Was it painful or even boring to hear someone's perceptions about them? Did they learn something from that process or was it just a waste of time?" Michael answered that it had set the stage for what followed. He appreciated that the conversation had taken place in front of them so they could clarify any misconceptions and comment on her comments.

It was particularly interesting to their therapist to work on a team with another foreigner and to note the impact of three distinct cultural backgrounds (US, French, and Norwegian), which created an opportunity for each to learn from the other: "By necessity there would be some generous giving in of initial perspectives and the couple was given the opportunity to see that too. With these differences to draw on, you must be more patient and willing to be more spontaneous." In her view, there is another process going on in the team itself, so that ideas don't stay fixed but continue to move and stay open.

While she was speaking, I mused that in conversation with people from foreign countries, you are aware at the outset that you speak different languages; you cannot automatically assume that you understand each other. It is necessary to listen very carefully and in so doing you begin to mutually create a language. Now listen, now reflect to see you understand, now talk – share your understanding of what you think the other is saying, but always with an element of not being quite sure. It forces you to make more room for different shades of meaning. When you both speak the same native language, it is easier to become "lazy" and assume you know what the other person is saying without the need for periodic checks.

It helps to continually share the picture one makes of another person's picture. I suppose what is ongoing is commentary on language, and deriving a language about language. And of course, there are limits of language – if my picture is too different from yours, I may misunderstand what you mean. This sensitivity and responsiveness to subtle shades of meaning are woven into the reflecting team.

New Stories

In the three months following the reflecting team consultation, new information surfaced – Michael had been keeping various secrets from his wife. When she happened to find out, it
felt like his father's "secret life" that came to light only after his
breakdown. As I listened to this new story, I recalled the question that had been hanging in the air during the reflections:
"Would it be necessary to go through such a big crisis as they
feared or could that grounding and connection be implemented
otherwise?" This prompted my questions about the impact of
this disclosure, "Was that a relief or was that a burden, or . . . ?"
and wondering whether they had taken any ideas with them
from the reflections. One idea had stayed with Laura – that
Michael could get help, and that they could become closer without his having to have a breakdown.

The effect of Michael's disclosure had been profound. It had
been freeing to him; in his "nakedness," he felt a burden lift and
a sense of being grounded.

M: I felt naked . . . this is it . . . this is what's happening
. . . it's all there and this is me. And I just felt like I
was hanging all out; I wasn't holding it all in or holding it together . . .
A: So there was nothing that you needed – to hide.
M: There was nothing to hide, there's nothing to hide
anymore.
A: Was that a relief or was that a burden, or – ?
M: – It was a major relief . . . starting over, from scratch,
with a blank slate.

Laura experienced an initial relief and a deep sense of valida-
tion of what she had been sensing and seeing, which had up to
that moment been denied. So, in a sense the problem they had
originally come in with had now dis-solved (Goolishian &
Anderson, 1987) by the act of *naming a problem they now can
both agree exists*. For Laura the difference was that Michael
now "*realized* it's a problem. . . . Before it was always *not* a

problem and *not* an issue, even though it obviously was." She felt as if she had just been through a long labor – with the final relief and exhaustion. She is quieter and has turned to herself, no longer needing to conduct a frantic search for answers from the outside; she is giving time for the conversation with herself to emerge.

Their private time is balanced by glimpses of connection, both within the couple and with the few people with whom they have conversed about the problem. They now sense an opening for exchanges of a different nature: now, after distancing, Michael comes back and talks to Laura about it. The relationship between him and his father has also begun to deepen, with father again being a father and Michael again being able to be a son. In his view, his father has become a good model, "in the way he's being a father and in the way he's listening, not making judgments . . . just being there for us." The disclosure has slowed things down, with enough time for both talking and reflection; a time of "letting go and letting come" (Andersen, 1987). There are glimpses of connection but a larger need to let things evolve over time.

This calls to mind fundamental questions about the nature of change. Do the problems or rather the questions the client comes in with change over time, and if so, how? Do the clients tell themselves that the problem is solved, or do they merely change their description of it? With this couple, the act of naming a problem in a different context – one that allowed for exchanges of a different nature – then invited new options, new descriptions and actions. What is the effect of allowing for conversations of a different character and quality to emerge: within self, with another? And how does each create or influence the other? These questions form the context for the next couple.

TWO SUNS

This couple, Karen and Daniel, told a story of transitions – a move towards togetherness with their recent marriage and a move toward separateness with an expansion of their two careers. In the reflecting team interview, they talked of moving out of a time of pain, struggle, and difficulty, of the breakup of a first marriage, of Daniel initially coming to therapy according to the terms of his probation. For the therapist, the question was how to balance the initial work with Daniel to make room for work with the couple.

Several questions surfaced in the afterwords interview: Is there room to expand? Is there room enough for two—for another point of view, another person, other connections, even for the notion of "problem"? For Karen, the present signaled an end to suffering and struggle, and a beginning of "readiness for change." Daniel was occupied by his wish for perfection and what he felt as imperfection and what it now meant if there were differences, disappointments, sadness or conflict.

The ideas this couple took with them from the reflecting team were generative—of new ways of looking at old situations and an awareness of different levels of conversation with self and others. In the afterwords interview, they commented on the nature of change—how they were now able to reflect on themselves and how this new process of conversation with self might create the opportunity for different conversation with others.

K: What's most memorable for me was the image that one team member gave of the two suns. He said that from . . . [the] first . . . , prior to our entering the session itself, he had the image of us both being like bright suns. And he elaborated on that as very positive. He had a very positive approach, no question; there was no criticism implied.

And at the same time it was apt for us because . . . most universes have only one sun, right? So who is the sun? And the tension that ensues from that.

So, it was that moment and that part that stood out most for me . . . it was this rather poetic image that seemed most valuable for me.

A: So you then had this image in your head of, could I create a universe with two suns? Or—

K: – That was my end – therein lies 50% of the problem!

A: Did it shift since then as to whether you could create a universe that is unique enough to have two suns or whether you would have a super bright one?

K: A super bright one or two? I think it's sort of leaning toward the two! Two have to mutually exist, and then can they exist in some kind of harmony or tension that's workable from day to day.

As we conversed, I had the image of a planet with two suns and wondered whether the picture she made had two suns or one sun that reflected the brightness of the two. This informed certain crucial questions for this couple: e.g., can there be room enough for two or only enough for one? Is there room for difference, in perspective, in background, in ideas? How do you make room for both one and the other, for his view and hers, for both harmony and tension?

Daniel recalled his feeling that there had been room for difference in the reflecting team meeting: he was impressed by the different backgrounds, ages, and perspectives that the team members brought to bear on the issues presented. As he described it, each had his or her own voice, whether "analytical" or "looking at the dynamics among people" or "describing the interaction from an artistic or aesthetic point of view." For him the image of the suns also evoked other pictures:

> the image of perfection which we may call a circle, a sphere, the sun. . . . And how one deals with issues . . . or intrusions into that perfection; . . . problems that could become issues of dysfunctionality, our fears or our unhappiness, sadness, sorrow, loss . . .

Jiminy Cricket

I wondered, what was the effect on this couple of listening to two, or three, or more perspectives? Did it have any impact on how they now talked to each other? Daniel had come away from the reflecting team with ideas which generated other ideas about how he might reflect differently on himself:

D: The ways in which we reflect on ourselves . . . that has been interesting to me because it's like having a Jiminy Cricket or a way in which you have another part of yourself looking at a particular way you're doing things, and be able to say, "Wait a minute, before I act in this particular way, maybe I can have other options here . . . "

Through some kind of very simple interjection of another perspective, maybe you can come up with another reaction in a particular situation dealing with another person.

A: So those would be two instances where it was almost generative, where the idea generated other ideas?

D: That's correct; it produced a kind of line of thought or action, or thought that could lead to action.

A: So it wasn't only generative in terms of other ideas, it was generative of ideas leading to actions.

D: Yes. I've used both of those two approaches in the intervening time . . . *I'm aware of being able to do that now.* What it gave me was a kind of new vocabulary or *language to be able to talk to myself,* to say "wait a minute," or "what about . . . ?" Or "it doesn't have to be perfect, let's take a look at what isn't perfect . . . "

It was really a vocabulary that was being developed. The interesting thing was, it was a vocabulary about two specific individuals, that is, Karen and myself. And, therefore, the images had a lot more personal relevance. . . . So, I felt it was the process in which you did have this focused attention.

A: So, it was something about their following very closely to what you were talking about?

K: Yes. For me it was the delicacy and the close attention and caring.

Language was mutually created by carefully following the words and pictures unique to each conversation. A language, or perhaps a dialect, was delicately built up over time by exchanges of vocabulary – both words and pictures, what was said and what may have been left unsaid. Daniel found that since that time he has been making pictures in response to those offered in the interview. Some can be described in words; others are still in the process of formation.

Karen had the overriding impression of a particular kind of atmosphere that allowed issues to be opened up, "a quality of the people involved that I would define by delicacy, gentleness, insightfulness, compassion." She felt that the initial process of conversation between the interviewer and their therapist had been very effective; it was a "point of entry" and a way of setting the stage for what followed:

K: You or I could stand back and listen and say, "oh, that's true" or "that's not true'" from my experience. Rather than . . . doing all the talking oneself . . . , you could say, "oh, that's not the way it is from my perspective."

A: So that gave you a point of comparison.

K: Yes. Which isn't to deny your experience . . . it's like all these different facets of a jewel, and my facet is this and you're seeing this facet.

Daniel went on to describe his reactions to the team's conversing about their conversation. He recalled that before the reflecting team meeting he had feared that it would be threatening and in actuality it never was:

D: I did have reservations and none of them became reality. It was . . . a whole bunch of people you never saw before . . . , and they're going to be talking about your life! My goodness, what's going to happen? (*laughter*) And, I said, just keep an open hand and just walk in! And that's exactly what happened; it was just a very positive interaction . . . and the whole thing was positive, and I wanted it to continue on!

I think the overriding benefit of it for me was that . . . it was opening up ways in which *myself, for myself,* I could be thinking about these issues in a nonthreatening way.

A: So, in a way it had an effect on the way you talk to yourself?

D: It had an effect on the outcome which was a process, and my willingness, my internal willingness. [I think] by presenting an interactive process in which the two people are incorporated on an equal basis, everybody has an opportunity to reflect, everybody has an opportunity to say something. And it doesn't appear to be hierarchical.

In the following portion of the interview, I was aware of the connection of different levels or aspects of conversation described by Daniel which overlap and touch each other in time: his internal conversation while listening to the reflecting team, then transferring the external (what he listened to in the reflecting team) to the internal (how he now talks to himself since the meeting); and finally, the connection between conversation with himself to conversation with others.

These conversations are reflexive – one influences and affects the other, providing new information. In addition, I was struck by the process of double or even triple description that he can now draw on to generate new choices of action.

Description of Listening to the
Reflecting Team → Internal
Conversation

Daniel described parts of the process that allowed him to begin to reflect on himself in a nonthreatening way. I wondered, what invited that exchange and what was it about the dialogue he had with others in the reflecting team that allowed him to have a different kind of dialogue with himself?

A: I am intrigued by the notion that somehow that way of talking then affects how you talk to yourself?

D: Yes. I think it's just transferring an external model to an internal one . . . part of the answer is the fact that there isn't just one perspective on who a person is. In other words, you have . . . many different perspectives on any one particular conversation so that what everyone comes away with is *their own particular perspective on that conversation. Even the totality of them isn't the conversation. . . . You can't ever get back to what the poet meant because he said it.* But you can have everyone's response to what that meant, what *they* feel it means.

This echoes the notion that the observer's point of view determines what is seen. You can never *know* truths; what you can do is compare the descriptions offered by others.

Conversation With
Self→Conversation With Other

In terms reminiscent of Bråten's (1987) notion of making room for another view, the "virtual or actual other," Daniel described the connection between his internal conversation and how that is reflected in the conversation with others. He described his own internal dialogue as reflexive; his ideas inform his actions which inform his ideas. For Daniel, the experience of making room for alternate views in the reflecting team and within himself also created the opportunity to do the same with Karen:

D: It then opens up a multitude of various responses. . . . The dynamic there is one in which I then begin to do the same process myself. In other words, . . . let us say I'm confronted with an issue, how am I going to respond? . . . I could respond in this way, but wait a minute, I have other options . . .

K: —you could take an analytic or a family or an artistic response—

D: — I could take my conversation and probably take a look at it from each of those perspectives. So it increases my vocabulary by three, four, five, ten fold — however many of these little voices, or images or perspectives I want to incorporate. It's ... a different way of coming at a conversation. ... How do we think, how do we respond to a question? It opens up other possibilities.

In another situation it may be confrontative; ... then, ... I can back off from that because I have other possibilities to respond to you. Maybe I don't even want to respond to the issue of the moment, maybe I just want to say something like "I love you," or "I understand what you're saying, I understand what it is and I don't have a good answer for you."

So it opens up other possibilities rather than, ... running in the same groove of that record. What I've become interested in is, I have run a lot of the same grooves of a record and the ruts have become very deep. And you lose a lot of good sound after a while.

Karen described the experience differently and emphasized her appreciation for "the opportunity to dialogue about intensive personal issues that Daniel and I have." In her view the questions asked opened up issues in a context that invited the couple to talk about them. In the couple's view, there was a lot of focused attention on specific issues and the concerns of each partner.

A: I'm wondering if there was anything that shifted your perspective on the initial questions you came in with even though it's ongoing?

K: I didn't come in with questions, so my questions didn't shift. What I came away with was this reminder that the best kind of ... work, is done in an affirmative setting rather than a critical setting. I tend to be very critical, which is a difficulty that I have in my relationship with Daniel.

A: So that gave you a way to put *criticism in parentheses*?

K: Criticism in parentheses. It's much better to work with an image like the sun that was offered, and say, that's got a lot of virtue to it – a sun! It also has its own problems, as a moon would, as a planet would – as any other image, as a daisy, would.

A: So it opened up a whole other way of looking at in, in a way?

K: Yes.

A: For you, Daniel, did you come in with questions that got shifted, or maybe you didn't [come in with questions] as Karen didn't?

D: (*pause*) My major question was how to get along with Karen better, and it did answer – give another way of viewing – that. I have other approaches to the questions that I have perceived, and the answers may be entirely different. Maybe they're not even answers, they're just approaches. . . . So it kind of put it in perspective.

This couple thought that the reflecting team gave room for issues to be opened up in an atmosphere that invited exchanges that were positive and not pejorative. And what was then the effect? Is the act of making room for problems like making space for another viewpoint – the "virtual other" or the "loyal opposition" (Bråten, 1987; Hoffman, 1988)? Is the new description or the process of making room then a step towards the dissolution of the problem, or a way to change its meaning (Anderson & Goolishian, 1988)? If so, they *no longer view it as a problem and, when they do so, it no longer exists as a problem.* There is the possibility for new alternatives.

COMMENTARY

The afterwords interview uses time as punctuation by providing a vantage point from which the couple can now reflect on themselves in context of the reflecting team, on the events that followed, and on the reflecting team process itself, creating multiple perspectives. Each recursion then gives another point of comparison on the issues or questions that organized the system initially. It puts the self and the reflecting team in a larger context of the events that preceded and the process that has evolved since. It is one way to follow up the reflecting team interview, one way to look at "outcome." A clear distinction between outcome and process relaxes; *outcome* becomes process and *process* becomes outcome.

Each of the afterwords conversation had its own form and character, but the four couples had some impressions in common of the reflecting team process. They had been profoundly affected by the opportunity to have professionals openly converse with each other in front of them. They could (and did) offer their own views as counterpoint, in the reflecting team and again in the afterwords conversation as *their own* statements and judgments about us. They described a positive atmosphere in which "expertise" was shared in a nonhierarchical manner, and in which the ideas of the client system were given equal weight. Expertise was no longer felt to be the exclusive province of an outside professional but expanded to include the client system. The locus of change became mutual inquiry.

I came away from the afterwords conversations with my own reflections – ideas and questions about language and its limitations. When words become building blocks and you no longer rely on the automatic use of language, you can shift to another level – that of conversation. I wondered, what is it about a conversation that invites dialogue, and how does the ability to have a dialogue within yourself create the opportunity to have a dialogue with another? And, at what point does the exchange of descriptions itself become dialogue and at what point does it lapse into monologue? There are other questions about the extent to which the afterwords conversations were influenced by my descriptions, ideas, and style. For the intention was not to merely conduct an "interview" but to continue the dialogue begun in the reflecting team. Indeed, there was a sense that another dialogue had begun as each couple spontaneously reflected on the "afterwords" interview and asked if perhaps the new conversation could be continued in the future.

I was struck by the creativity of the couples' descriptions of the reflecting team process. There were several levels of description or multiple reflections: between client and professional; between speaker and listener; within self and between self and other. And the narratives changed as they were re-constructed over time – a process of double or even multiple description. Ideas generated other ideas and pictures were painted in response to images offered. Metaphors had been used and exchanged in the reflecting team and the afterwords conversations. And this started me wondering to what extent it is personal style and to what extent the reflecting team invites the use of metaphor by its emphasis on respect, sensitivity, and imagination. Perhaps its structure mirrors the language of choice of those in conversation, or perhaps metaphor indirectly or implicitly addresses a "problem." Maybe the process of reflecting opens a door between what is known and what is not yet formed, carefully following the ideas of the client system and also introducing small differences. This reminds me of Koestler's (1975) remark that metaphor is but another pathway to provide a slightly different viewpoint that may connect two previously disparate or unknown frames of reference and thereby create perspective.

Metaphor is one kind of description, one way to carefully follow how meanings develop in conversation. It is a most vivid illustration of the constructive nature of language, as it demands an investment in social process where we are reminded of the way meanings are created. This creative process may then collapse the duality of either one view or another to embrace the possibility of both . . . and. The reflecting team builds on this notion and a willingness to entertain the uncertain world of neither . . . nor. In this exercise in subtle invitation, new connections are as available to the speaker as to the listener. As Bateson (1980) reminds us, metaphor may provide a triangulation on the known and a link to the unknown.

7

THE REFLECTING TEAM AND THE INITIAL CONSULTATION

William D. Lax

Although the reflecting team model (Andersen, 1987) is fairly new, it has already been incorporated into a wide variety of clinical contexts. This chapter describes its utilization in initial interviews. A description of this type of consultation and a case example will be presented.

Therapists and theoreticians in the field of family therapy have recognized the role and importance of the initial interview in therapy and numerous descriptions of intake procedures have been developed. The literature endorses a variety of different approaches, including defining problems distinctly at the outset of therapy (Haley, 1976), formulating and revising goals and hypotheses (Selvini Palazzoli, Boscolo, Cecchin, & Prata, 1980; Weber, McKeever, & McDaniel, 1985), joining the family system (Minuchin, 1974), and encouraging the therapist to be active and directive in the session and to be thoroughly prepared prior to the interview (Bryant, 1984).

While the reflecting team model follows some basic approaches and assumptions which have evolved in family thera-

My appreciation to Tom Andersen and Lynn Hoffman for their valuable assistance in the development of my thinking and to Sydney Crystal, Judy Davidson, Dario J. Lussardi, Dusty Miller, and Mardie Ratheau for their contributions to earlier drafts.

py, particularly those of the Milan associates, it reexamines some of these ideas and offers both new thinking and procedures for the initial interview (see Andersen, 1987; Lax & Lussardi, 1988; Miller & Lax, 1988).

HISTORY OF TEAMS AT BRATTLEBORO FAMILY INSTITUTE

When staff at Brattleboro Family Institute first began to work as a team in 1982, we set aside one morning and one evening a week for team cases. Initially we tried to see as many cases as possible with a team. We were quickly overwhelmed with too many team cases and had to change our approach.

Our next phase was to attempt to "screen" cases to see which ones would be appropriate for this time slot. This screening was very arbitrary, based on a decision at the time of the initial telephone call whether the case might be a "difficult" one or not. We found that many cases which we thought would be best seen by a team were "easy" ones and ones that were screened out were "difficult" and could have used a team.

We finally arrived at our current procedure. We see as many couples and families as possible in a reflecting team format for an initial consultation and at the end of the consultation decide with the clients whether the team will remain involved or not. In some instances this consultation process continues for up to three sessions. In a majority of the cases the team does not remain directly involved with the case after the consultation, and the interviewing therapist continues alone.*

---

*On some occasions the team will stay involved with the case, and this decision will be based on both the team's ideas and the clients' desires. The team will stay involved when some of the following conditions are present: the therapist is experiencing some discomfort with the case or does not feel she has a good understanding of the clients' view; the system is very complex, with multiple outside/larger systems involved; there are multiple "paradoxes" or continual disqualifications taking place in the system and the therapist feels easily "lost"; the team has a particular interest in the clinical material; or the initial team is a training team and has made a prearranged decision to continue with this case, following it to its completion.

The Interview

Our initial interview makes several departures from established formats. These include the following: having a pre-session meeting that focuses on the *format* of the interview rather than on any clinical hypotheses; having the interview address the *context* of this meeting rather than immediately discussing the content or "problem"; and considering this first meeting as a consultation, with future therapy being only one of many possible outcomes (Caillé, 1982).*

The therapist conducting the initial interview maintains the perspective of providing a context for new ideas to develop (Davidson, Lax, Lussardi, Miller, & Ratheau, 1988). It is assumed that families/social systems come to therapy with narratives or multiple pictures of their situation. These narratives are intertwined within a myriad of meaning systems carried by the individual members. The therapist enters the interview, as best as she can, without any fixed or predetermined story or hypothesis. She attempts to form an understanding of the family's picture(s) and meanings and, through conversation and reflections, hopefully to generate a new image that is not too different, but different enough to make a difference. At the end of the interview she then sees if the clients' narrative has changed in any way. The clients may have a different enough picture and/or another solution, besides therapy, has become apparent to them so that future therapy may not be desired or indicated.

The Telephone Contact

Contact with the clients begins with the first telephone call. In keeping with Anderson and Goolishian's (1988; Anderson, Goolishian, & Winderman, 1986) ideas about problem-determined and problem-organizing systems, efforts are made to determine what is the system of meanings or "meaningful system" (Imber-Coppersmith, 1985) from the very first contact

---

*This way of thinking and working, as described earlier, does not necessitate a team. Our work is merely one example in which a team is utilized.

with the clients and to invite those people to the first session. Thus, the therapist who receives the initial call asks, "Who is involved with this situation?" rather than "Who is in your family?" The possibility of all involved participants coming to the meeting is discussed, and the team format is described. The caller is told the following:

> We generally meet with new clients for a consultation to get a picture of their situation. This consultation usually takes from one to three sessions. I say "we" because, if it is acceptable to you, we like to work as a team for this consultation. What we generally do is have a therapist meet with you and interview you. This interview is observed by one to three colleagues who are actually watching and listening to the meeting in another room behind a one-way mirror. They do not talk behind the mirror. At some point in the interview you and your therapist will change places with them. For example, if I were meeting with you, after about forty minutes you and your family (husband/wife/mother/child) and I would go into the other room and my colleagues would come into our room. We would then watch and listen as they discuss their ideas about your situation and offer suggestions about how to proceed in the future.
>
> After they finish, which is usually in about five to ten minutes, we will go back into the room, and they will return to the other room. We then talk about their ideas and see which of them, if any, seem useful to you.
>
> The purpose of this method is to generate as many ideas about your situation as possible, including how to address the issues and what to do regarding future conversations and meetings. Does this sound acceptable to you?

If the caller does not wish to have a team observing, we offer to meet with them with two therapists in the room (T. Andersen, personal communication, April 27, 1986). If this method is still unsuitable to the caller, we offer a meeting with them with a single therapist only.

Just prior to the interview, the team meets without the family to inform all team members about the information received in the initial telephone call and to decide which therapist will meet with the clients.

*History of the Idea of Coming
to Therapy*

When the clients arrive, we gather some initial data concerning names, dates of birth, insurance information, etc. After this, the therapist discusses the format of the interview again with the clients. If there are any concerns, they are addressed at this time along with any changes in format. Clients are never forced to have a team involved with them.

This model relies heavily on thinking from social constructionism and constructivism and focuses on an examination of the clients' contexts and the meanings that they ascribe to their situation (see Gergen, 1985; von Glasersfeld, 1984). Thus, the next phase of the interview begins with a discussion of their *ideas* about coming to therapy (Andersen, 1987; Hoffman, 1988). The therapist asks questions regarding the context of this first meeting: "How did the idea to come to therapy come about? Who had that idea first? Who agreed the most/least with it? If you had that idea in the past, how do you explain that you did not come in then?"

This process allows us to engage in conversation with the clients "where they are" and not impose any predetermined ideas, formulas, or hypotheses upon them. Starting in this manner, at this semantic/meaning level, we are also interrupting the expected process and marking this meeting, from the very start, as different from their usual ways of addressing and thinking about their situation. In addition, we maintain the assumption that problems exist through the use of language by an observer saying "this is a problem" (see Anderson & Goolishian, 1988; Anderson, Goolishian, & Winderman, 1986). To ask "What is the problem now?" may only further reify the clients' already existing beliefs. This view allows the therapist to more fully understand how the stated problem(s) are intertwined in the clients' meaning system, their ideas about therapy itself, and the context of this particular meeting.

As the interview progresses around the history of the idea of coming to therapy, the conversation moves naturally to a discussion of the problems as defined by the clients. Problems are addressed when they arise in the interview and are not ignored. However, our primary focus is on the meanings that people ascribe to "problematic" behaviors and the language they use in this description. We assume that there is a recursive relationship between meanings and behavior. Thus, our emphasis or punctuation is on facilitating new meanings for the clients; as new meanings arise, the possibility for new behaviors increases. This is done through conversation with the clients, using questions and reflections during the interview (see Hoffman, 1988; Penn, 1982, 1985). Through the process of alternating questions and reflections in the interview, a new picture may eventually emerge for the participants (including the therapist), leading to a dissolution of an earlier conceptualization of the dilemma. This folding over of ideas is a continual process, with each comment and idea building from an earlier one. The therapist's job is to engage with the clients as best she can so that they can tell their individual and collective narratives in the context of *this particular conversation*. In addition, the therapist and/or team may offer a new perspective or difference, which is not too discrepant from the clients' preceding views to "make a difference" to the participants. This different perspective is not intended to replace the client's story with a "better" one, but possibly to add an alternative to their story. This process may then allow for a tension to be generated between the two versions, potentially offering both something new and/or an integration of this different perspective and other stories already developed (see Lax, in press).

The interview proceeds only as quickly as the participants can go, neither too slowly nor too fast for them to remain connected. Throughout the interview attention is given to who can be talking with whom, about what, and how (Andersen, personal communication, October 27, 1987). Our intention is to maintain the therapeutic conversation and not continue in a manner that is too different from the clients' style, pace, or willingness to proceed. If the conversation were to be either too similar or too different from their usual mode of interaction and understanding, the conversation might come to a halt.

When a new topic is raised by someone, questions are first

asked "about talking about" the topic rather than the issues themselves. For example, in a situation where someone raises drinking, we might first ask, "What would it be like if we were to discuss drinking now? If we were, who would have the most difficulty/ease discussing this? How do you explain that this would be difficult for them? With whom, if anyone, would they have an easier time discussing this issue?" (see Lussardi & Miller, 1991).

Also included in this phase of the interview is a discussion about anyone else who may have ideas about the dilemma who could be included in future discussions.

Reflections

Our initial interview usually lasts about one and a half hours. At some point in the interview, usually after forty to sixty minutes, the conversation will reach a natural pausing point or conclusion. The team members can then comment on the interview, introducing ideas of their own.*

Reflections follow some general guidelines (see Andersen, 1987; Lax, 1989). These center on presenting comments within a positive or logical framework as opposed to a negative one, moving from an either/or position to a both/and or neither/nor position, presenting a "smorgasbord of ideas" versus correct "interpretations," and offering ideas not as rigid explanations but as tentative thoughts.†

---

*In the absence of a mirror, the team members may be in the room with the client system, maintaining an imaginary boundary between themselves and the clients. With only two therapists both may wish to be in the room, having one remain silent during the interview and then "reflect" with the interviewer. The central importance is to maintain the talking and listening positions as discussed earlier by Andersen.

†While the shift to a neither/nor position may seem to resemble the either/or dilemma of the client, it is one in which, within the client system, neither one member's story nor another's is considered to be better. It is a shift to a different perspective in which a new story is introduced or co-constructed by the team or client system. This new version may be an integration of other stories or it may be an entirely new one.

The team may also raise comments and questions that the therapist did not or contextually could not say in the interview. These may include comments on "difficult" topics, such as alcohol/substance abuse, suspected incest or violence, and individual team members' subjective ideas or concerns which were not raised or addressed during the interview. By introducing these issues with the family observing and listening, the team allows these ideas to be present in the room, like "sky hooks," as a potential part of the ongoing conversation. The family and therapist then have the possibility of addressing them in ways that had not been available prior to this. This process allows the therapist to maintain her "proximity" to the client system and still explore these other issues (Lax & Lussardi, 1988).

Comments on the Reflections by the Client System

After the reflections, the therapist and clients switch back to their original places and the therapist usually asks each person some variation of the following questions: "Did you have any thoughts or ideas while you were watching and listening and what ideas seem to make sense to you? Was there anything that they should not have talked about or that you disagree with? Was there anything else that they should have included?" The first two questions are generally asked to determine what "fits" for the clients. The last question is particularly important because the clients may have begun to develop a new story or picture of their situation and are generating new solutions which were not thought of prior to the interview. This question gives them the opportunity to explore these with the therapist.

After the clients have fully responded, the therapist can introduce ideas of her own. Often clients do not respond to many of the reflections offered. These reflections are not viewed as irrelevant, nor are the clients seen as "resistant": the reflections merely do not fit at that moment. They may be "stored" by the therapist for possible use in the future, or they may come up again in clients' conversation.

As the clients respond to the reflections, the therapist can see if any new pictures or meanings have developed. The end of the interview folds back on the system's original ideas regarding therapy and questions future directions: Has a new picture/ understanding emerged that may not require therapy? If there are to be future conversations, the therapist and clients then need to reexamine who might talk with whom, about what and how in order to facilitate the continuing therapeutic conversation.

CASE EXAMPLE*

Mrs. Robbins called requesting an appointment for herself and her eight-year-old daughter, Molly, who was having "stomachaches" every morning and night and occasionally was not able to go to school. When I asked her who else she thought might be included in the interview, she said that she and Molly's father, Mr. Gable, were divorced, both had remarried, and she wished to come alone with her daughter. She told me that her current husband was concerned about the situation, but he worked nights and slept during the day, so he would not be able to come. I explained how we worked as a team for an initial interview and she agreed to this format.

I began the session with some basic questions about family members' names, ages, insurance coverage, etc. Mrs. Robbins, who was 33 years old and four months pregnant, said that she also had a three-year-old son. She explained that she and her ex-husband had joint custody of Molly: Molly spent the weekdays at mother's house and three out of four weekends at father's. Molly responded to my initial questions in a very engaging manner, and smiled and joked with me immediately. I then asked, "Whose idea was it to come to therapy, and who agreed with this idea?" Mrs. Robbins explained that the guidance counselor at Molly's school had suggested that they come for counseling after Molly had missed several days of school and

*The team for this first interview consisted of Judy Davidson and Dusty Miller.

that both she and Molly agreed with him. Molly said that she was "nervous being here" and sat next to her mother during the first part of the interview playing with a toy.

Mrs. Robbins described how Molly had been having stomachaches for the past three months and often did not want to go to school. Molly agreed with her mother and said that they happened "every day, even on weekends." I asked her what the stomachaches were like, she said that they felt like "one hundred tight knots" inside of her on "fourteen thick ropes." I gave her a jacket and asked her to show me how tight they were, and she rolled the jacket into a ball, saying that they were "the worst" in the morning. Mrs. Robbins said that she neither gives in to Molly when she has her stomach problems in the morning nor ignores her. She tells her that she can "lie in bed during the day while Mom is at work, but cannot go out and play."

I realized that Molly had used the word "knots" instead of stomachaches, so I adjusted my language: "I realize that I have been asking you about stomachaches and you have been talking about knots! Tell me, how are these knots different at your mother's house and your father's." She said that the knots were "more and tighter" at her father's house; when she left her father's home the knots got looser. She did not have any explanation for this difference. When I asked what explanations Mrs. Robbins had, she said that she had made a "mistake" recently by moving the family back to the house that they had lived in before the divorce and that there were "too many shadows in the closets." She also believed that the divorce itself had impacted upon Molly. She explained that her ex-husband had been having an affair during their marriage, had said that it had stopped, but continued to see the other woman (whom he later married). When she discovered that he was still seeing this woman, she left the marriage. Mrs. Robbins added that drinking was also one of the issues that led to their divorce.

Molly had been following the conversation closely, and I asked her what she thought of her mother's explanations. She said that her father did not drink anymore, as he had not had anything to drink for the past two weeks. However, she said what does bother her is that "he did not say goodbye, but just left." It seemed that when Mrs. Robbins confronted Mr. Rob-

bins about the affair continuing, he just left without any explanation to Molly. Mrs. Robbins said that she tried to explain to
Molly what happened, but Molly has never heard her father's
side.

I asked Molly about her relationship with her father, and she
said that it was "OK." Mrs. Robbins said that several weeks
earlier Molly had requested a change in the visitation schedule
that would allow her to spend more weekend time with her. Mr.
Gable told Molly that he believed that her mother had "put her
up to this request" and he would not even consider it. Mrs.
Robbins explained that when he does not want to talk about
something he yells. Later, he will complain to her that Molly
doesn't talk with him about what is bothering her. Mrs. Robbins explained that Molly is a "sensitive child," that she and
Molly are very close and talk a great deal together, and that she
encourages Molly to "express her feelings."

At this point we had been talking for about forty-five minutes, and the conversation had reached a lull. I suggested that
we see if the team had any comments, and we switched rooms
with them.

Reflections

The team began their reflections with one member comment-
ing on the caring and closeness between the mother and daughter, and how Mrs. Robbins had clearly given much thought to
this dilemma. She then said that while she was watching she
had an image of the "knots wanting to tell people something:
Does Molly know what they might be saying? Would she feel
safe telling what the knots have to say or should she keep it a
secret?" The other team member said, "The knots might have
many, many things to say, to many different people, but particularly to her Mom and Dad." She was "surprised that there are
not *more* than a hundred knots." She also wondered "if there are
other messages that the knots might have for Molly." She was
impressed with how loyal she was to her Dad, wanting to support him with his trying to stop drinking and imagined that
she was probably very sad when he left. "Molly is so good at
protecting her parents – were the knots also trying to protect
her parents from something that might be said?" The first

team member then continued with some thoughts about the difficulty saying goodbye, particularly when Molly's father did not say goodbye to her. She wondered if the knots may be "company" to her at the transition times between mother's and father's homes. They finished with a brief discussion about how we did not know what the knots were saying or doing, that we needed to find out more from Molly about them, and that we wondered if it was safe for Molly to talk more about them here.

Response to Reflections

After we switched rooms, mother responded first saying that the team "hit it right on the mark. I have always told Molly that it is not good to hold it in, whatever it is, even if it is anger." When I asked Molly what she thought about the team's comments, she said that she "didn't know."* I gave her a brief summary of the reflections and asked her if she agreed with anything that was said. She said, "Some of it." I asked if she "thought that the knots have things to say." She responded, "No." I asked, "If you didn't have the knots, do you think that you would have more things to say?" She responded, "Yes." When I next asked her who she might say these things to, she did not respond. I decided that I had asked her one too many questions about the knots at this point, but continued, "May I ask one more question about our meeting?" and she said, "Yes." "Would you like to come back and talk again, and if you did, would you like to come alone, with your mother, with your father, or with both of them?" She said that she would like to come back, but with her mother only, and added, "I'm not nervous anymore."

The Second Interview

They returned for the next session two weeks later. At this meeting Judy Davidson was the only team member observing.

---

*We have found that young children and/or teenagers often say "I did not hear what was said" or "I don't remember." However, usually they have been watching very intently during the reflections. The therapist can remind them what was said and often they will respond to these prompts.

Molly started talking immediately and said that she had "thought more about the knots . . . I can tell you what they look like. They are so small that they look like a piece of string." I asked, "Is it possible that sometimes you don't even notice that they are there?" "Yes." Mrs. Robbins interjected that Molly had not complained of any stomach problems during the two weeks between sessions and had not missed any school. She then asked Molly if she remembered that "we had a talk in the car and you told me how you are scared to talk to some people?" Molly said, "I'm kind of scared to talk with my Dad." We talked about how difficult it was for her to talk with her father and about her wish to spend more weekend time with her mother.

Reflections

After about forty minutes Judy came out from behind the mirror and had a conversation with me in front of Mrs. Robbins and Molly. Our conversation included the following comments: "While talking here has helped with the knots, I wonder what talking with Dad would be like? Would talking with Dad make things better or worse? For the time being the knots are gone. If Molly begins to talk more with Dad, will the knots return? Are we trying too hard to encourage them to have that conversation? Should we take a wait-and-see position and not meet for a few weeks and let them decide?

After these reflections Mrs. Robbins spoke first: "We *all* believe things are not going to change unless her Dad is involved in this. I would like to do it in this setting. In the past talking always resulted in a three-ring circus. Perhaps this could be different." Molly then said that she would like to talk to her Dad. I suggested that Molly come back once more and we "practice" telling him what is on her mind so that this time could possibly be different. She immediately agreed. I asked them if they thought we could meet without a team next time, and they said that that would be fine.

Our consultation was now over. The reflections at the end of the first meeting began, as they often do, focusing on some positive dimension of the interview, in this case the relationship between mother and daughter. The team members then introduced ideas and questions pertaining to the knots, how the conversation might proceed in the future, who could be included in these conversations, and at what pace. A metaphor was developed surrounding the "knots" related to their size, shape, and the messages to which they might or might not be connected.

This new story began with Molly's introduction of knots instead of the term "stomachaches" and my emphasis on it. Mrs. Robbins added to it with her focus on the value of expressing feelings. The team furthered this process by introducing ideas about the knots being a form of communication. After the first session, Molly had a "reflection" of her own to her mother in the car, expanding the narrative: She connected the knots directly with her fear of communicating with her father.

The reflection during the second interview introduced the idea that there were thoughts and feelings that were both expressed and unexpressed that Molly may want to address to her father. We were then able to "talk about" what it would be like if Molly were actually to talk about them with him. The reflection did not mandate that she act in this manner; it was only a suggestion to consider. A direction was agreed upon by all members of this therapeutic system and the course of a future conversation was established in which all members could participate.

Follow-up

When we met two weeks later, Molly was still experiencing no knots. With her mother in the room, Molly and I spent the time making a list of what she wanted to tell her father, still without any commitment to presenting it to him. It included the following:

1. When I feel sick I want to go home to Mom's.
2. I love you, even when I want to go home.
3. I am afraid of you when you yell.

At this meeting we again discussed what it might be like to tell her father what was on her list, and she and her mother decided to invite her father to the next session.

Mr. Gable came to the next session. Initially he was very gruff, as he had no idea why he was invited. He soon became more responsive when we talked about Molly's stomach problems and some of the ways that we had been talking about them. He agreed that her stomach problems were also of concern to him. I finally asked him, "What would it be like for you if your daughter had some things to tell you about herself and you?" He said that he would like to know what his daughter had on her mind. Molly stood up and asked him if she could tell him what was on her "list." He said yes, and she read it, saying the first two items quickly and then slowly saying "and I am frightened when you yell at me."

After a brief silence, her father said that he knew that, and asked her if she could be patient with him. He was trying hard to deal with his alcohol problems and knew that when he gets mad at his wife he takes it out on Molly. He told her that he loved her and hoped that she could give him another chance. They hugged, and he cried.

Mrs. Robbins watched quietly. Since the parents had said earlier in the session that they get along well now, except for when they have to talk about Molly, I suggested the possibility of my meeting with them to talk about these occurrences. The parents agreed to come without Molly. On the day of that meeting, Mrs. Robbins called and canceled the appointment because of an illness. She later phoned and said that she did not want to meet with her ex-husband at all, and that Molly was doing fine. At follow-up calls six months and one year later there were no further stomach problems.

The therapy raised a central question for us: If the "problem" was over, when does therapy stop? Clearly, to us the stomach problem had stopped after the second interview, but we all felt that it might be important to assist Molly in addressing her father. The stomach problems had been framed as keeping her from telling him something. Without them she was able to talk, but she needed some support to do that. While we had further ideas about the direction therapy could take regarding the interactions between the parents and presented these to them, Mrs. Robbins was very satisfied that her daughter's stomachaches had ceased and that Molly had spoken clearly to her father. Mrs. Robbins did not want to continue in therapy with him, as she felt that the situation was no longer a problem.

SUMMARY

Use of the reflecting team model in the initial consultation offers the therapist and family numerous benefits. Both have the advantage of making decisions about beginning treatment with a broader range of ideas. If further therapy is chosen, ideas presented at the initial consultation can be utilized by the entire therapy system, since these are available to all of them. Therapy becomes both client and therapist focused, with an emphasis on what fits for the system at any particular moment in the conversational life of the treatment system. The therapist is able to begin any future treatment from a nonhierarchical, lateral position, respecting and empowering the clients and their beliefs. Thus, therapy starts in a collaborative manner, rather than with the therapist seen as the expert and the clients seen as "sick."

When a team has participated in the initial consultation, a therapist continuing to work alone with the family has the team available for continuing consultation/supervision. The team can also be readily reintroduced should the therapy reach an impasse. In addition, working as a collaborative, noncompetitive team helps us avoid professional "burn-out" and allows us continually to share our clinical work and ideas with one another. But perhaps the single most significant benefit is that clients often report that they feel "understood and respected" at the beginning of therapy.

8

REFLECTING DIALOGUES IN SUPERVISION AND TRAINING

Judith Davidson
Dario J. Lussardi

OUR EVOLVING TRAINING MODEL

Our initial training programs were strongly influenced by the Milan associates and their team approach. While we had experimented in our clinical work with strategic, structural and MRI techniques, the Milan approach seemed to "fit" with the collaborative, non-hierarchical aspirations of the team and, over time, a systemic orientation emerged as the preferred theoretical framework. An additional influence on our training model was Lynn Hoffman, who initially was a clinical consultant to the staff of the Brattleboro Family Institute and later joined the Institute as a senior faculty member.

An incentive for our establishing training programs was our enthusiasm for the team approach and the wish to do more teamwork, utilizing this approach in a cost-effective way. Many people had touted the benefits and advantages of teamwork only to dismiss it as inefficient and impractical, a luxury available only in large, urban training centers. Because our training programs were funded primarily by the students' tuition, training teams provided us and the community the added bonus of being able to offer therapy for reduced fees to families who might not otherwise have been able to afford it.

All programs included both didactic and experimental components and live interviews were conducted using a one-way mirror. In this model, students learned from observing the trainers and other students, as well as from their own experience as the therapist in the room. An additional benefit of using teams was that the many ideas developed in team discussions helped students develop systemic hypotheses and understanding more quickly (Campbell & Draper, 1985). As we continued to evolve, we discovered that it was not sufficient to just teach and demonstrate to our students how the method and techniques worked. Instead we found it useful to engage with trainees in a process based upon the ideas of second order cyberneticians like Heinz von Foerster, Humberto Maturana, and Francisco Varela (Hoffman, 1985; Keeney, 1983). This meant that we had to abandon the notion that we were the "experts" who would impart knowledge and understanding upon our students. Instead we participated in conversations in which we, trainers and trainees, would co-construct an understanding, taking into consideration the assumptions and beliefs held by both trainees and trainers alike.

Though this process, we found that greater attention had to be given to each student's ideas about therapy and change, previous training experiences, and current work setting. Doing this meant that we were spending less time "teaching" and more time being curious about students' ideas, their agencies, and their work with clients. The use of circular questions was invaluable in this process. In effect, we were "modeling our model" of therapy in our teaching. Recently, other authors have emphasized the need for mutual respect within a training program so that a trainee does not feel caught in a covert or overt battle between the ideas taught in the training program and the ideas she has already developed or the ideas and methods of her workplace (Lebow, 1987).

As we were experimenting with being less "expert," we began to question other elements of the model. One concern reflected the necessity of narrowing down the multiplicity of ideas discussed in the intercession to just one or two which then would become the essential elements embedded in the intervention delivered to the family. Because of our theoretical beliefs and our practical experience in using "O-teams" and "T-teams" (Boscolo & Cecchin, 1982), we were aware that several different hypotheses and interventions were possible for the same family dilemma and we emphasized this to our trainees. However, practicality required an eventual reaching of consensus. The very necessity of doing this sometimes introduced a covert sense of competition as well as the notion of one idea being better than another. More experienced therapists with a particular viewpoint sometimes found it difficult to be open to new information and tended to become wedded to their views, resulting in some very uncomfortable intercession "battles." In addition, beginning therapists sometimes were "overimpressed with the ideas of a supervisor" (Boscolo, Cecchin, Hoffman, & Penn, 1987) and stifled their ideas in deference to the supervisor/trainer. We found this to be particularly awkward in training situations in which the therapist in the room was the trainer, viewed by all as the "expert."

Having been impressed with the use of the reflecting team model as a clinical tool, we decided to incorporate this approach into our training programs. In doing so we found that we could avoid these dilemmas since all ideas are potentially "useful."

For example, we once provided a consultation for a training team which was stuck with a family partly because of these hierarchical issues. The therapist in the room was the clinical director of the agency, a very respected clinician. The team members, all trainees or junior therapists, had joined the team specifically to watch him work and to learn from him. The family consisted of a mother, father, and four sons, one of whom was developmentally disabled. Over the course of the therapy, the therapist became very connected to the family and began to see the situation almost as if he were one of the sons. The team members had different views and would call in their ideas and questions. Although the therapist would verbally agree with the team, he was never able to express the team's question or point of view in the way the team had intended. The team members, however, felt constrained from pushing their ideas because the therapist was the "expert." In the course of the consultation we learned that, on one occasion, the team had been successful in presenting a different point of view, an intervention which all agreed had been instrumental in helping the family move in a new direction. This had occurred when there was a female on the "team" who was a senior supervisor and thus was perceived to be on a more equal hierarchical level with the therapist/clinical director. The consultants, in their reflections, were able to comment on the dilemmas of each part of the family/therapist/team system that had led to the difficulties in introducing new information. With these dilemmas out in the open, the system was able to develop some new possibilities for therapy. However, it is our belief that the use of the reflecting team model would have lessened, if not eliminated, some of the hierarchical dilemmas between the trainer and the team.

Before we routinely used the reflecting team format in our training programs, questions had also arisen for us around how to handle the issues of power and control that occasionally came up between trainers. Because the emphasis of Milan-style teams is generally on a non-hierarchical organization and on collaboration, there is no easy way to resolve a deadlock between team members (Boscolo, Cecchin, Hoffman, & Penn, 1987). One situation which served as the initial catalyst for our use of the reflecting team occurred when there was a difference of opinion between two trainers about what should be the central punctuation in the formulation of a particular intervention. The disagreement between the trainers was awkward for the trainees as well as for the co-trainers. It was exacerbated by the fact that one trainer was a more senior member, yet the more junior member had a longer history with some of the trainees. This created a potential loyalty dilemma for the therapist/ trainee in the room and the team. As a way of surmounting this impasse, they decided to do a reflecting team and presented the family with all their ideas. They were delighted with the family's response to the reflecting team's conversation and felt that this model was a way of helping the trainers, trainees, and family members move to a place "beyond power and control" (Hoffman, 1985).

DISCOVERIES

In introducing the reflecting team approach to our training groups, we were immediately struck by the fact that this was a way of doing therapy which enabled all trainees to be more directly involved in the clinical work and to have a presence in the room. We had long struggled with trying to find a way to provide opportunities for trainees to be more included in the therapy process. Usually the bolder, more outgoing trainees would volunteer first, leaving fewer chances for others to be the actual therapist in our time-limited program. This approach allowed even the shy trainees to have direct input in the room and in front of the family and their colleagues. The reflecting team model seemed to truly equalize team members by giving them the opportunity and responsibility to provide feedback to the family and therapist.

Since then, we have discovered numerous other benefits for our students in using this model. First, we think that this approach fosters greater autonomy in the therapist/trainee because she does not go into the session with a set of hypotheses to explore that have been predetermined by the team. Instead, she is free to follow the family's lead and becomes more skilled at responding to the feedback from the family. If the therapist does feel stuck or runs out of questions, she has the security of knowing that she can always ask if the reflecting team has any ideas to offer. Although all students are usually anxious about conducting first interviews in front of their peers, we have found that students tend to develop confidence in their interviewing skills more quickly, perhaps because they are not interrupted. Moreover, just as students learn that there is no "right" solution or intervention for the family, so they come to see that there is no "right" question to ask; consequently, they seem to worry a little less about their performance.

When we first started using the reflecting team model in our training programs, we were concerned about whether trainees new to this approach would say something negative about the family and whether they would be able to reduce the wealth of information presented by a family in an interview to a few salient points. We addressed some of these fears by having the students engage in numerous role plays in which they alternated between being members of the reflecting team and members of the family. When acting as reflecting team members, students had the chance to practice articulating what was most striking to them in a session and how to phrase these ideas in ways that might be useful and non-blaming. As members of the family, they had the opportunity to experience how powerful an experience it is to be in a "listening" position and to hear others converse about you. They could also provide feedback to their peers about what sorts of reflecting team comments were helpful or not, thus increasing the sense of collaboration among trainees and lessening the tendency to view the trainer as the "expert" upon whom all were dependent.

An extra benefit of the reflecting team model has arisen from the rule of "no-talking" behind the mirror among team members. This rule was originally developed in order to increase the number of ideas presented to the family and to decrease the possibility that team members would eliminate some ideas through discussion. We have discovered that a side effect has been that it has fostered a more genuinely respectful attitude towards the family because it forced the trainees to keep negative remarks about the family's behavior to themselves.

APPLICATIONS IN OTHER TRAINING SESSIONS

Having been pleased with the results of this model within our "in-house" training programs and having developed some videotape examples of this work, we began to experiment with these ideas in other teaching and training contexts. In our graduate classes on family therapy, we have found it to be quite useful to divide students into reflecting teams and then to have them observe a portion of an interview on videotape. Each team "reflects" as though the family were listening. We then show the original reflections on tape and discuss how ideas were formulated within each team, including similarities and differences. This method provides students with an opportunity to examine their thought processes and to practice relating these thoughts in ways that might be useful to families.

We have also used this model in our consultation to other agencies. One family therapy team operating within a community mental health center requested ongoing consultation for their team with a stated goal of becoming a more cohesive group. While acknowledging that they had different backgrounds, training, and views of family therapy, their desire was to become an effective therapeutic team. The group included clinicians from different departments and with different areas of specialization, e.g., child abuse, adults/couples, intake, evaluation and testing. They also had different levels of experience and different hierarchical positions within the agency. Some had been supervisors to others.

As we began to work together, it became apparent that these differences, and possibly others which were not recognizable to an outsider, showed up as power struggles, some of which were more obvious than others. For example, it seemed that the position of being the person who telephoned messages to the therapist was a position of status. Being relegated to the "O-team" also held lesser status. Jokes were made about being on the "out" team because it was perceived that this role was less important and had little impact upon the course of therapy. Sometimes pre-session and post-session discussions would become competitive when hypotheses were being formed or when we were choosing areas to explore. Some therapists might be more inclined to ask questions about the past, while others might want to know more about how people behave in the present or about how they envision themselves in the future.

When we introduced the reflecting team approach, these dilemmas were solved. There was no need to phone in, there were greater opportunities for more therapists to have direct input into the therapy process and the "O-team" reflections upon the team's conversations gave them a greater role. Most importantly, room was created for all ideas to be expressed, thereby hon-

oring all the different perspectives as equally valid and potentially useful to the family.

USING THE REFLECTING TEAM IN SUPERVISION

We have also found it useful to incorporate this approach
within our supervision groups. As a staff, we rely upon each
other for consultation around clinical issues in our weekly peer
supervision meetings. We also offer consultation to other therapists in supervision groups. Obviously "stuckness" is not a
state exclusively reserved for our clients and we therefore apply
the same principles in dealing with the impasses in our work.

With the advent of the reflecting team, we are now experimenting with a new format: having only one member of the
supervision group interview the therapist about the case while
the other members later reflect. Instead of encouraging the
therapist to present a narrative of her views (which might lead
to the team's accepting her definition of the problem, her construction of "reality"), the interviewer starts by asking questions such as:

"What concerns led you to want to discuss this case?"

"What dilemmas do you face in your work with this family,
couple or person?"

"What understanding or explanations do you have about
these dilemmas?"

The interviewer continues with additional circular questions
and, as this is occurring, the others listen silently while generating their own thoughts and questions, which are then reflected back to the therapists and interviewer. The therapist
then has a chance to comment upon any ideas that she finds
interesting. Sometimes the two-person interview/discussion
will then resume and sometimes there will be a discussion
among all group members.

Thus far, we have had very positive reactions to this model.
First, the therapist being interviewed does not have the sense
of being bombarded by questions from many colleagues all eager to participate and be helpful. The circular questioning by
one person has more continuity and the therapist feels less

pulled in different directions. The nonjudgmental, tentative reflections also allow for the broaching of potentially awkward
issues, such as whether there is some connection between the
case and the therapist's own life or whether there are other
potential isomorphs. The therapist being interviewed feels less
defensive because she does not have to respond directly to any
of the reflecting team's comments but rather is free to respond
to whatever she wants.

CASE EXAMPLE

During one supervision group at another agency, two colleagues, a man and a woman, wanted ideas from the group
about how they could best proceed in their work with a couple.
Roger had originally seen the couple together but, after three
sessions, the wife, who was recovering from her second cancer
operation, decided not to continue in couple therapy for the
time being. Instead she asked to see a female therapist for
individual sessions, citing a need to work on her own issues.
Roger agreed to refer the wife to a female colleague, Maggie,
who had extensive experience with cancer patients. The husband wanted to continue seeing Roger individually until the
couple therapy resumed. Because of the husband's anxiously
intrusive style, the two therapists decided it would be important to maintain clear boundaries around the separate individual therapies.

The husband at first had encouraged the wife's separate
therapy. However, as he became increasingly desperate about
the marriage, he began to tell Roger that his wife was "lying" to
Maggie and began anxiously pushing Roger to tell the husband's side of the story to Maggie so that she would have the
"full picture." He also began complaining to Roger that his wife
was doing certain things because "Maggie told her to do it,"
which made Roger feel protective of Maggie and her reputation
as a therapist. Under these conflicting pressures, Roger tried to
talk to Maggie about how the therapy with the wife was going
and questioned whether couple therapy should be resumed.
Maggie, who had just learned that the wife had been sexually

abused as a child, felt even more strongly that the wife's boundaries should be respected and experienced Roger's questions as
a violation of the boundaries around her therapy with this client. She believed that, given the wife's life-long experience of
being violated and intruded upon, the wife needed to be the one
to decide when to re-engage in couple work. She felt strongly
that it would be a therapeutic mistake to push the wife into
couple therapy and told Roger this. She also wondered if, in a
covert way, Roger was questioning her competence as a therapist.

Maggie turned to another staff member, a woman, for several informal consultations about the case. Roger also talked
with this woman in an attempt to clarify his concerns and
perhaps gain her support for renewing couples therapy. The
female colleague viewed what was happening between the two
therapists as isomorphic to the couple's "dance," pointed this
out to Roger, and wondered why he was pushing so hard for
couple therapy when, ordinarily, he would view this as a choice
for the couple to make jointly. She also wondered if he might
deal with the husband's anxiety differently if the wife were
seeing a therapist who worked in a different agency. Although
Roger acknowledged that he wouldn't, he was frustrated with
the two women colleagues' ideas because he still felt that the
husband had no "voice" or way of influencing his wife.

A crisis developed when the wife began to have suicidal
thoughts. Both therapists became very anxious and asked to
present the case at the staff's supervision group. The consultant decided on the following format: he would first interview
the female colleague who had been consulting to both Maggie
and Roger and then ask questions of them; finally, the other
staff members, who had been involved in the case, would form
the reflecting team. It was hoped that this process might generate new information about the relationship between the two
"couples." The colleague was asked numerous circular questions
about her role and perceptions, such as:

"How did you become involved in this case? How would you
describe the dilemma from Roger's and Maggie's perspectives?
Is it similar or different? How do you see the connection be-

tween Maggie and the wife? How do you see the bond between Roger and the husband? Are there any similar issues between Maggie and Roger? How do you explain Roger's frustration? Does the fact that Roger felt he was not 'heard' by the two female staff reflect any underlying gender issues within the staff?"

Other questions focused on how the potential suicide might create anxiety in each therapist and whether any larger systems were involved. Maggie and Roger were able to add their ideas and comments as the interview progressed.

A significant amount of information was generated in the interview: both the wife and the female therapist had had cancer; the husband and the male therapist both had similar ways of dealing with anxiety and similar styles; the relationship between the two staff members had originally been a hierarchical one when the female therapist had been an intern three years previously but had been changing as she gained confidence in her own ideas and skills. The relationship between husband and wife, forged when the wife was recovering from her first cancer operation, had also originally been a hierarchial one in which the wife was totally dependent upon the husband for nurturance and support. However, the wife's need for the husband to be a caretaker had lessened as she had become very successful at her job. The threat of suicide created additional issues: a previous patient of the woman therapist had killed herself recently and Roger was concerned that the husband, angry at the individual therapist anyway, would sue if the wife hurt herself.

Following the interview, the other members of the supervision group reflected upon all these multiple levels and views while their colleagues listened. In their comments, they were able to highlight both the similarities and differences between the couples which, in turn, helped the therapists make clearer distinctions between themselves and the couple. Maggie, who up until this point had been powerfully caught up in the similarities, described listening to this part of the reflecting team as especially helpful. She was suddenly clearer about all the ways in which she and Roger were not like the couple. For

Roger, who was feeling that he had made a "mistake" by becoming inducted into the husband's viewpoint, listening to the reflecting team's comments without having to respond directly made him feel less defensive. He felt that his position had been "heard" and understood, and was struck by the reflecting team's idea that his "intrusiveness" stemmed from his protective concern for Maggie. The reflecting team also raised some interesting questions about relationships among all the staff. For example, a question about whether the disagreement on this case reflected underlying gender issues (because the male staff person had felt unheard by the two female staff), led to a unique conversation about how individual staff members expressed anger and frustration to each other.

CONCLUSION

Thus far we are very excited about our uses of the reflecting team in supervisory and training contexts. This model, in its varied forms, has provided greater consistency within our therapy and teaching models. Trainees and supervisees have responded positively to a more collaborative model and have found it useful to their clinical work. The feedback has been enthusiastic and encouraging. In particular, the generation of ideas and possibilities for engaging in therapeutic conversations in a respectful, collaborative fashion has been appreciated. Furthermore we have enjoyed utilizing this approach which, in and of itself, generates enthusiasm for our work. We see this as an evolving model.

PART III

Further Reflections

EPILOGUE:
REFLECTIONS ON THE BOOK
TWO YEARS LATER

Tom Andersen

The period between October 1987 and December 1988, when this book was originally written, was very stimulating. The writing clarified many of my thoughts, changed some of them, and actually made new thoughts emerge.

It is very interesting to read the book today, in February 1991. It would undoubtedly have been different if it were written now. Some of it would have been omitted, some of it emphasized more, and some of it expanded. And I would have added other material. Now, as the text is being re-edited, I have been given the opportunity to indicate these eventual differences. This chapter will therefore replace the original final chapter, "Ending This Book is a New Beginning."

WHAT I WOULD HAVE OMITTED

I definitely would have taken out the words *explain* and *explanation*. These words belong, as I see it today, to that part of the world where the physical sciences exist (d'Andrade, 1986). In that part of the world one searches for descriptions that hopefully represent exactly the physical phenomenon one studies. By studying and describing the phenomenon under different influences, one might be able to *explain* what produces which change. One might even be able to *predict* how the phenomenon will be changed if it is influenced by this or that. Based on such studies one might develop general laws of explanation and prediction for the actual phenomenon and similar phenomena, which in turn can be used to regulate and control the surrounding world – or at least part of it. This kind of science and its corresponding language fit well in that part of the world where the "inner life" has a very slow rate of turnover – actually, where the movements of the inner life are so slow that it looks as though the element is dead. A piece of metal, for instance, changes very slowly; it might take decades for a human eye to see any change.

The world that we who use dialogue as a "method" for change work in is composed of living people and their meanings. This world encompasses both how they can understand themselves and the world that surrounds them and also their meanings about how they can take part in that world. People and particularly their meanings change all the time, and those changes happen very rapidly. Meanings are manifold and shift with shifting contexts. Meanings can hardly be explained in the sense that their causes can be indicated. Neither can meanings be predicted.

It is also impossible to describe what the meanings "really" are. Meanings cannot be steered nor can they be controlled, and there are of course no general laws that might guide our understanding of how meanings might be explained and controlled. We can never come closer than our *attempts* to understand others' meanings and thoughts. I can never come closer than *my* understanding of the other's understanding.

However, in the midst of being sorry to have used the word *explanation* in the first edition of the book, I am a bit relieved to notice that its content leans towards the word *understanding*. Nevertheless, if I had written the book today, the words *explain* and *explanation* would have been replaced by *understand* and *understanding*.

WHAT I WOULD HAVE EMPHASIZED

There are three issues I have in mind.

The first is the idea about organizing a meeting such that the participants are given opportunities to shift between actively participating in talking about one or more issues and listening to others' talking about the same issues. These shifts make it possible to go back and forth between the outer and inner dialogues. These two different kinds of dialogues will give two different perspectives on the same events and will also provide two different starting points when we search for new descriptions and understandings. I hope I have conveyed to the reader the idea that such shifts can be organized very differently: sometimes with the use of a team, sometimes in collaboration with only one colleague, and sometimes only with the clients, for instance, members of a family, present. In the last case those who listen while the therapist talks with one of the family members become reflecting participants and maybe later become "a reflecting team."

The second issue concerns the four main questions I work with during a conversation. The first of these is: "How would you like to use this meeting?" This question, which comprises both how and what, might be phrased differently according to the situation, e.g.: "Have you made any plan how . . . ?" or "Do you have any idea how . . . ?"

The second of the four is: "What is the history of the idea of coming here today?" This question might also be phrased differently, e.g.: "Who had first the idea . . . ?" "How did the various others become acquainted with the idea . . . ?" and "How did they like the idea . . . ?" The idea behind this question is to reach an understanding about how much those who are present are committed to the idea of being present. I am inclined to let those who are reserved about being present sit quietly and listen to my conversation with those who are more committed. The answers of the engaged ones to the question, "How would you like to use this session?", are carefully noted, since those answers will serve as the major frame for the meeting. This second question comes most often at the beginning of the session, but not necessarily. It might come later.

The third question, which is sometimes raised only to myself but might also be raised in the open, is: "Who can (ought to) talk with whom about this issue in which way at this point in time?" One should never take it for granted that everybody present can talk with everybody else about whatever may emerge during the talk. Therefore, when a new issue is brought up, it might be wise to ask: "How often have you talked about that before?" If this is the first time, it might be a good idea to ask who might talk with whom in which way now.

The fourth question I ask only of myself: "Is what we are talking about or is the way we are talking about it appropriately unusual or too unusual?" Those with whom we converse will give signs when they feel uncomfortable. We should encourage ourselves to notice those signs as early as possible in the meeting. Every person has his or her personal signs. If those signs emerge, I see it as my job to find something else to talk about and/or to talk differently.

At this point in time I am very much occupied by the third of the three issues, namely the importance of letting a person talk undisturbed until she or he has finished talking and of allowing the little pause for thinking that always follows. Later in this chapter I will say something more about this in relation to the attempts to define *self*. That discussion fascinates me.

WHAT I WOULD HAVE EXPANDED

I would have used a few words to point out that shifting reflecting positions can be used in various settings where many persons are present around the same theme or task, e.g., supervision, staff meetings, work with development of organizations, etc. This can be easily done by dividing those present into groups and letting one group discuss while others listen to them and later letting those who listened talk with each other about what they thought as they heard the first group talk. Then the first group again has a chance to talk.

Consultations of one therapist who works alone to another who does the same are another topic that deserves attention. One such single working therapist could ask a colleague to come to her or his office for a meeting, e.g., once or twice a month. The guest therapist might talk with the host therapist for a while about the therapy the client(s) and the host therapist have done so far, with client(s) in a listening position. Thereafter the guest therapist might talk with the client(s), with the host therapist in a listening position. Then the two therapists might reflect together, with the client(s) listening to that. Finally, the whole would end with a talk with the client(s). The two therapists might take turn being host and guest.

WHAT I WOULD HAVE ADDED

Here I would have tried to clarify where the "outer" process, which became part of participating in various reflecting processes, has brought me. I would have tried to describe what the components of this "outer" process were and how it contributed to changes in the way I practice and understand "therapy."

Now, as I try to share the thinking around this "outer" process, I will do so in terms of *me, mine, my,* and *I.* I want to underscore that *what* I share might be of significance solely for myself, in the sense that this "what" is framed by my language and my background. Another person might have defined the contributions differently. It is probable that the "what" I myself have found will not contribute to any general knowledge. However, in sharing "what" I have found the contributions to be, I will try to clarify *how* these "whats" were reached. And maybe that *how* will be of more general interest.

I find it interesting in hindsight to notice that the practical changes came first, followed by the ideas about how they could be understood. It might be useful to point out what the various practical changes were before talking about what contributed to them. The various changes will be summarized chronologically as they appeared over time: a shift from being ignorant of being too unusual to being aware of being so ("Am *I* appropriate or too unusual *now*?"); the shift from an either/or to a both/and stance; conducting all talks during a meeting in the "open," making them "public" so to say; encouraging multiple descriptions and understandings of the same; the leaving out of hy-

potheses; discussing *with* the clients what their commitments
were to participation in a meeting with us ("What is the history
of the idea of coming here?"); discussing *with* them how we
should talk together ("How would you like to use this meeting?"); ignoring the understanding of clients as parts of social
structures, social patterns, and so on, and instead concentrat-
ing on understanding the mode and content of their conversations with others' and with us, the professionals; discussing
with clients which conversations they might find useful in the
future ("Who might talk with whom about this issue in which
way at this point in time?"); simplifying the procedure of a
meeting as the repertoire of shifting reflecting positions expanded; giving increasing attention to *how* the clients express
themselves in addition to listening to *what* they talk about; an
increasing tendency to search with them for "un-heard and un-
seen" lights and shadows in their language; paying more attention to myself as a listener, listening carefully to which metaphors they use and being aware of the speed and rhythm and
pauses and force of talking by which they express themselves;
being a listener such that the other can talk undisturbed until
s/he has finished talking and the small pause that always follows; and the not yet seen changes which I believe have already
occurred.

What contributed to these changes?

What seems to stand out most is the significance of *my*
feeling of *uneasiness*, particularly when this feeling emerged
during a meeting and lasted after the meeting was over. That
feeling stirred the question: "What happened that made me feel
so uneasy?" I can see in hindsight that this feeling was re-
pressed and not taken seriously for quite some time. That happened during the period when I felt excited by understanding
what the pattern of a family was and, based on that, applied
various attempts to change the pattern—explanations or advice or tasks or more-or-less surprising reformulations, etc.
What often happened after such meetings was that the feeling
of uneasiness emerged. One day, however, that question—What
happened in the meeting that made me feel so uneasy?—
pushed for an answer.

I have always preferred to take long solitary walks to search for such answers. Walks in an area composed of contrasting elements are most useful. Up here where I live we might walk for hours in the mountains seeing the ocean out there at the same time. The eyes are given great differences to look at, so they could easily stop and glance, but I have noticed that they don't stop on such searching walks. They tend to move all the time – until an answer is found.

I assume the reader is well acquainted with the so-called "rapid eye movements" that correspond with the periods of dreaming during sleep at night. Maybe the reader also shares my perception that those who are convinced that their understanding and solution are best and right look confidently toward fixed points in front of them. Those who are more uncertain, maybe so uncertain that they feel confused, tend to move their eyes in searches for something to fixate. Eye-fixers and eye-movers.

I cannot exactly recall now what came first to mind: Gregory Bateson's idea about "a difference that makes a difference" or Aadel Bülow-Hansen's nuancing it to "there are two differences that make no difference, but one (the appropriate different one) that does." Both ideas were connected to a rethinking of an ongoing relationship as a flow of givings and takings. I came to understand my uneasy feelings as a signal that this flow was experienced as too slow or too quick. The feeling of uneasiness came most often when the flow was felt to be too slow for me and I pushed it to be quicker, while the others felt it uncomfortably quick and wanted to decrease and even stop it. On such occasions, I could sense my pushing attempts. That feeling of *pushing* someone who for his/her part resisted the push felt uneasy. I asked myself, how should I handle such uneasiness? Should I ignore it, e.g., by saying, "This is part of therapy"? Should I take it seriously, asking, "Do I want to be in such relationship to others?" I chose to answer no to both.

What has been interesting since making this choice has been noticing that the feeling of uneasiness in various relationships has stimulated major changes in the way I work. Actually, all the changes mentioned above come from such wonderings about feeling uneasy. What is the basis for that feeling of being uneasy in a relationship? While I have no "objective" answer to that, I have devoted much thought to it. Part of the proposed answer to myself is that it is based on, in Hans Georg Gadamer's terms (Warnke, 1987), my pre-understanding of what a relationship is (shall be). If so, it comprises elements both from my general cultural background and from my local cultural background; it is historical and contextual and therefore constantly shifting. It becomes a shifting personal "standard," not a stable and general one. Whatever its basis, I know how it feels and let that feeling guide my participation in any relationship.

I see recognizing that feeling to be part of intuition. Intuition is in my terms a state of being open to the "answers" from "inside" myself when I am "touched" from "outside." The touches from "outside," such as those that occur in a relationship, reach the eyes, ears, and skin. If I am open to and take in the touches, there will be "answers" from "inside" myself which tell me how to respond to the touches. One of the answers from inside of which I am particularly aware is the pushing.

In pursuing this lead, it has been interesting to notice that Gareth Morgan (1983), a well recognized researcher in the field of human sciences, emphasizes that research in the human realm basically involves modes of engagements to others. Various changes in my practical work have been much stimulated by feeling uneasiness in various situations. The changes themselves seem to represent a new understanding of conversation and constitution of self.

Prior understandings of constitution of self were connected to structure. A person's expressions were seen as depending on the underlying structure, either biological, psychological, or sociological (e.g., a family). The professionals' corresponding takings and doings tended to be *to* and *for* the clients. We now talk *with* the clients and do various things *with* the clients. A person is seen first of all as a participant in conversations.

The next natural step was to focus on the language used through conversations. At the Galveston Family Institute's*

---

*The institute is now called Houston-Galveston Family Institute.

conference in Galveston, Texas, October 25-26, 1988, Harry
Goolishian delivered exciting ideas on just this point:

> Why is it that these changes in thinking are moving so rapidly
> and how come at this time? How come the theories of construc-
> tivism are now flourishing, and in so many different areas of the
> arts and sciences? How can we give meaning to these changes?
> Is there a direction? How is it that so many of us are dulled and
> disenchanted with our current aesthetics and our current prac-
> tice? How come our theories and institutions seem so tar-
> nished? How come at this time? These and many other ques-
> tions roar into my head as I ponder this meeting and the
> overwhelming response to a small invitation.
>
> In wrestling with these questions and in thinking about our
> area of mutual interest, the social sciences and psychotherapy, I
> thought of Ludwig Wittgenstein and his comments on the role
> and importance of language. I also thought about the emphasis
> a number of philosophies place on the central and problematic
> role of narrative discourse in understanding the human situa-
> tion. This includes such giants as Alysdair MacIntire, Richard
> Rorty, Paul Ricoeur, Jean-Francois Lyotard and others. A major
> thesis throughout Wittgenstein's writing is that the limits of
> our language furnish the limits of our world. A constant thrust
> in the writings of the narrative philosophies is that the limits of
> our narrative structure, our genres, and stories define our abili-
> ty to understand and explain. Our prevailing narratives provide
> the vocabulary that sets our realities. Our destinies are opened
> or closed in terms of the stories that we construct to understand
> our experiences.
>
> This view of narrative and vocabulary has, of course, major
> implications for our work in psychology, psychotherapy, and the
> social sciences. Within these areas of study, according to the
> narrative view, we have only our descriptions. These narrative
> descriptions are our understanding of the nature of humankind.
> These descriptions and stories are in continuing evolution and
> change. To conclude that the views of human nature are only a
> matter of our language conventions, only a matter of how our
> stories and narrative genre relate experience is to say that our
> fictions are the only nature we know. This is a sobering thought.
> Can it really be that what we conclude about the basic core of
> human nature, the things we know about ourselves and others,
> what it is that we ourselves are can all be reduced to functions of

the language and the narrative plots available to us? Are these what set the boundaries of our sociological and psychological sciences? Can it be so that any understanding we have, all our descriptions of the world, the very ways we observe social organization, the tools through which we understand problems, the modes through which we do therapy are all nothing more than expressions of our language use, our vocabularies, and our stories? Is it our semantics through which our actions achieve meaning? Even more awesome, are the implications that our human agency, that complex set of operations through which we take knowledgeable action in our lives and coordinate and organize ourselves with others, nothing more than transformation into action of the narratives that we co-create with each other? The linguistic position is a firm yes. Our very selves, our agency, our institutions, our law, our order, our very civilization are nothing more than a fictional expression of our language use, our vocabularies, our fictions. A few small examples – it would be impossible to think of such complex social activities as an insanity defense or depth psychotherapy without the narrative and vocabulary of the unconscious. Without this word to describe our behavior, this and many other important rituals and social organization would be senseless. It would be impossible to think of love, cooperation, power, or romance without the appropriate language to describe these actions. We would not live the way we do if we did not talk about it the way we do. Without the vocabulary of love it simply would be impossible to engage in romantic relationship. Without the language of power we could not oppress each other. Without the language of hate we could not hurt each other.

These ideas lead to an understanding that talking is much more than being informative. The act of talking certainly involves giving information to others, but it is something more, namely constitution of self during the self's way of expressing her- or himself. In other words, through talking a person searches for the metaphors that best *express* the person's understanding and opinions, and this is done in a way that contributes to the person's expressing her/himself. Gergen (1984, 1989) and Shotter (1989) have contributed much to broadening these perspectives.

Meetings with Aadel Bülow-Hansen and her successor, Gudrun Øvreberg, have given me the opportunity to understand the bodily participation in a person's expressing her- or himself. All that is expressed, either words or emotions, goes by the exhaling phase of breathing. The movements of breathing are very sensitive to shifts according to what is expressed and the contexts in which the expressions occur. Therefore, being a listener involves not only giving attention to the words and metaphors and meanings that are expressed but also being aware of and avoiding disruption of the physiological part of talking – the speed and rhythm and pauses and force of voice. Being such a listener, one offers the other a co-search for the other's constitution and re-constitution of her- or himself. Or, more colloquially, one might say: being with the other such that the other becomes the person she or he wants the most to be in that situation at that moment.

An interesting overall discovery has been that practical changes occurred first; these were followed by attempts to understand the changes; then I have been ready to discuss the various processes within theoretical frames. I can see today that the theoretical frame that appears in this book from two years ago is somewhere between the natural and the human sciences. If such a theoretical frame were to have been written today, it would lean more towards the human sciences. Although my understanding of the reflecting team and the reflecting processes has changed, the clinical work basically remains the same. Investigating this change of understanding might be my next project. It also might remind us that practices perhaps inform and change our theories more often than theories influence our practice.

REFERENCES

Andersen, T. (1987). The reflecting team: Dialogue and meta-dialogue in clinical work. *Family Process, 26*(4), 415–428.

Andersen, T., & Katz, A. (1987). Letter to clinical colleagues.

Andersen, T., & Naess, I. (1986). Four hearts and four patients in dilemma. *Family System Medicine, 4*(1), 96–106.

Anderson, H., & Goolishian, H. (1987). Menschliche Systeme. Vor welche Probleme sie uns stellen und wie wir mit ihnen arbeiten. In L. Reiter, E. J. Brunner, & S. Reiter-Theil (Eds.), *Von der Familientherapie zur systemischen Perspektive.* Heidelberg: Springer.

Anderson, H., & Goolishian, H. (1988). Human systems as linguistic systems. *Family Process, 27*(1), 3–12.

Anderson, H., Goolishian, H., Pulliam, G., & Winderman, L. (1986). The Galveston Family Institute: Some personal and historical perspectives. In D. Efron (Ed.), *Journeys: Expansions of the strategic-systemic therapies.* New York: Brunner/Mazel.

Anderson, H., Goolishian, H., & Winderman, L. (1986). Problem determined systems: Towards transformation in family therapy. *Journal of Strategic and Systemic Therapies, 5*(4), 1–11.

Atkinson, B. J., & Heath, A. W. (1987). Beyond objectivism: Implications for family therapy and research. *Journal of Systemic and Strategic Therapies, 6*(1), 8–17.

Bateson, G. (1972). *Steps to an ecology of mind.* New York: Ballantine.

Bateson, G. (1978). The birth of a matrix, or double bind and epistemology. In M. E. Berger (Ed.), *Beyond the double bind. Communication and family system, theories, and techniques with schizophrenics.* New York: Brunner/Mazel.

Bateson, G. (1979). *Mind and nature: A necessary unity.* New York: Bantam.

Bateson, G. (1980). Workshop presented at the Boston Family Institute.

Bateson, G., & Bateson, M. C. (1987). *Angels fear: Towards an epistemology of the sacred.* New York: Macmillan.

Blount, A. (1985). Towards a "systemically" organised mental health center. In D. Campbell & R. Draper (Eds.), *Applications of systemic therapy: The Milan approach.* London: Grune & Stratton.

Boscolo, L., & Cecchin, G. (1982). Training in systemic therapy at the Milan Center. In R. Wiffen & J. Byng-Hall (Eds.), *Family therapy supervision.* New York: Basic.

Boscolo, L., Cecchin, G., Hoffman, L., & Penn, P. (1987). *Milan systemic family therapy.* New York: Basic.

Bråten, S. (1987). Paradigms of autonomy: Dialogical or monological? In G. Teubner (Ed.), *Autopoiesis in law and society.* New York: EUI Publishers.

Bryant, C. (1984). Working for families with dysfunctional children: An approach and structure for the first family interview. *Child [Adolescent Social Work Journal, 1*(2), 102–117.

Caillé, P. (1982). The evaluation phase of systemic family therapy. *Journal of Marital and Family Therapy, 8*(1), 29–39.

Campbell, D., & Draper, R. (Eds.). (1985). *Applications of systemic therapy: The Milan approach.* London: Grune & Stratton.

Cecchin, G. (1987). Hypothesizing, circularity, and neutrality revisited: An invitation to curiosity. *Family Process, 26,* 405–413.

Christiansen, B. (1972). *Thus speaks the body.* New York: Arno Press.

d'Andrade, R. (1986). Three scientific world views and the cove ring law. In D. W. Fiske & R. Shweder (Eds.), *Metatheory and social science.* Chicago, IL: University of Chicago Press.

Davidson, J., Lax, W. D., Lussardi, D. J., Miller, D., & Ratheau, M. (1988). The reflecting team. *The Family Therapy Networker, 12*(5).

Gergen, K. J. (1984). Theory of the self: Impasse and evolution. *Advances in Experimental Social Psychology, 17,* 49–115.

Gergen, K. J. (1985). The social constructionist movement in modern psychology. *American Psychologist, 40*(3), 266–275.

Gergen, K. J. (1989). Warranting voice and the elaboration of the self. In J. Shotter & K. J. Gergen (Eds.), *Texts of identity.* London: Sage.

Gergen K. J., & Gergen, M. (1988). Narrative and the self as relationship. In L. Berkowitz (Ed.), *Advances in experimental social psychology.* New York: Academic Press.

Goolishian, H., & Anderson, H. (1987). Language systems and therapy: An evolving idea. *Journal of Psychotherapy, 24*(3), 529–538.

Haley, J. (1967). *Advanced techniques of hypnosis and therapy: Selected papers of Milton H. Erickson, M.D.* New York: Grune & Stratton.

Haley, J. (1973). *Uncommon therapy.* New York: Norton.

Haley, J. (1976). *Problem-solving therapy: New strategies for effective family therapy.* San Francisco: Jossey-Bass.

Hansen, V. (1987). Psychiatric service within primary care. Mode of organization and influence on admission-rates to a mental hospital. *Acta Psychiatrica Scandinavia, 76*, 121-128.

Hoffman, L. (1985). Beyond power and control. Toward a "second order" family systems therapy. *Family Systems Medicine, 3*(4), 381-396.

Hoffman, L. (1988). A constructivist position for family therapy. *The Irish Journal of Psychology, 9*(1), 110-129.

Imber-Coppersmith, E. (1985). Families and multiple helpers: A systemic perspective. In D. Campbell & R. Draper (Eds.), *Applications of systemic theory: The Milan approach*. London: Grune & Stratton.

Keeney, B. P. (1983). *Aesthetics of change*. New York: Basic.

Koestler, A. (1975). *The act of creation*. London: Picador.

Lax, W. D. (1989). Systemic family therapy with young children and their families – Use of the reflecting team. *Journal of Psychotherapy and the Family, 5*(3/4), 55-74.

Lax, W. D. (In press). Postmodern thinking in a clinical practice. In K. Gergen & S. McNamee (Eds.), *Social constructionism and therapeutic process*. London: Sage.

Lax, W. D., & Lussardi, D. J. (1988). The use of rituals in families with adolescents. In E. Imber-Black, J. Roberts, & R. Whiting (Eds.), *Rituals in families and family therapy*. New York: Norton.

Lebow, J. (1987). Training in family institutes. *Journal of Family Psychology, 1*(2), 219-231.

Lipchik, E. (1988, Winter). Interviewing with a constructive ear. *Dulwich Centre Newsletter*.

Lussardi, D. J., & Miller, D. (1991). A reflecting team approach to adolescent substance abuse. In T. Todd & M. Selekman (Eds.), *Family therapy approaches with adolescent substance abuse*. Needham Heights, MA: Allyn & Bacon.

MacKinnon, L. (1988, Winter). Openings: Using questions therapeutically. *Dulwich Centre Newsletter*.

MacKinnon, L., & Miller, D. (1987). The new epistemology and the Milan approach: Feminist and sociopolitical considerations. *Journal of Marital and Family Therapy, 13*(2), 139-156.

Maturana, H. R. (1978). The biology of language: The epistemology of reality. In G. Miller & E. H. Lennenberg (Eds.), *Psychology and biology of language and thought*. New York: Academic Press.

Maturana, H. R., & Varela, F. J. (1987). *The tree of knowledge*. Boston: New Science Library.

McCarthy, I. C., & Byrne, N. O. (1988). Mis-taken love: Conversations on the problem of incest in an Irish context. *Family Process, 27*, 181-199.

Mendez, C. L., Coddou, F., & Maturana, H. R. (1986). Bringing forth of pathology: An article to be read aloud by two. Instituto de Terapia Familiar de Santiago.

Miller, D., & Lax, W. D. (1988). A reflecting team model of working with couples: Interrupting deadly struggles. *Journal of Strategic and Systemic Therapies, 7*(3), 17–23.

Minuchin, S. (1974). *Families and family therapy.* Cambridge, MA: Harvard University Press.

Morgan, G. (1983). *Beyond method.* Newbury Park, CA: Sage.

Øvreberg, G., & Andersen, T. (1986). *Aadel Bülow-Hansen's fysioterapi.* Tromsø.

Penn, P. (1982) Circular questioning. *Family Process, 21,* 267–280.

Penn, P. (1985). Feed-forward: Future questions, future maps. *Family Process, 24,* 299–311.

Segal, L. (1986). *The dream of reality: Heinz von Foerster's constructivism.* New York: Norton.

Selvini Palazzoli, M., Boscolo, L., Cecchin, G., & Prata, G. (1980). Hypothesizing – circularity – neutrality: Three guidelines for the conductor of the session. *Family Process, 19,* 3–12.

Shotter, J. (1989). Social accountability and the social construction of "you." In J. Shotter & K. J. Gergen (Eds.), *Texts of identity.* London: Sage.

Tomm, K. (1987a). Interventive interviewing: Part I. Strategizing as a fourth guideline for the therapist. *Family Process, 26,* 3–13.

Tomm, K. (1987b). Interventive interviewing: Part II. Reflective questioning as a means to enable self-healing. *Family Process, 26,* 167–183.

Tomm, K. (1988). Interventive interviewing: Part III. Intending to ask lineal, circular, strategic, or reflective questions? *Family Process, 27,* 1–15.

von Foerster, H. (1979). *Cybernetics of cybernetics.* New York: Gordon & Breach Science.

von Foerster, H. (1981). *Observing systems.* Seaside, CA: Intersystems.

von Glasersfeld, E. (1984). An introduction to radical constructivism. In P. Watzlawick (Ed.), *The invented reality.* New York: Norton.

von Glasersfeld, E. (1988). The reluctance to change a way of thinking. *The Irish Journal of Psychology, 9,* 83–90.

Warnke, G. (1987). *Gadamer, hermeneutics, tradition and reason.* Stanford, CA: Stanford University Press.

Watzlawick, P., Beavin Bavelas, J., & Jackson, D. D. (1967). *Pragmatics of human communication.* New York: Norton.

Watzlawick, P., Weakland, J., & Fisch, R. (1974). *Change: Principles of problem formation and problem resolution.* New York: Norton.

Weber, T., McKeever, J. E., & McDaniel, S. H. (1985). A beginner's guide to the problem-oriented first family interview. *Family Process, 24*(3), 357–354.

White, M. (1988, Winter). The process of questioning: A therapy of literary merit? *Dulwich Centre Newsletter.*

INDEX